HIGH THEORY/LOW CULTURE

HIGH THEORY/LOW CULTURE

MIKITA BROTTMAN

HIGH THEORY/LOW CULTURE
© Mikita Brottman, 2005.

First published in 2005 by
PALGRAVE MACMILLAN™
175 Fifth Avenue, New York, N.Y. 10010 and
Houndmills, Basingstoke, Hampshire, England RG21 6XS
Companies and representatives throughout the world.

PALGRAVE MACMILLAN is the global academic imprint of the Palgrave Macmillan division of St. Martin's Press, LLC and of Palgrave Macmillan Ltd. Macmillan® is a registered trademark in the United States, United Kingdom and other countries. Palgrave is a registered trademark in the European Union and other countries.

Library of Congress Cataloging-in-Publication Data

Brottman, Mikita, 1966–
High theory/low culture/Mikita Brottman.
   p. cm.
   Includes bibliographical references (p.) and index.
   ISBN 1–4039–6640–0 (alk. paper)
   ISBN 1–4039–6641–9 (pbk. alk. paper)
   1. Popular culture—History—20th century. 2. Civilization, Modern—20th century. 3. Popular culture—United States—History—20th century. 4. United States—Civilization—20th century. 5. Criticism. 6. Bakhtin, M. M. (Mikhail Mikhaélovich),1895–1975—Contributions in criticism. 7. Barthes, Roland—Contributions in criticism. 8. Lacan, Jacques, 1901—Contributions in criticism. I. Title.

CB427.B75 2005
306'.0973—dc22   2004050856

A catalogue record for this book is available from the British Library.

Design by Newgen Imaging Systems (P) Ltd., Chennai, India.

First edition: January 2005
10 9 8 7 6 5 4 3 2 1

Printed in the United States of America.

Contents

LIST OF FIGURES

Acknowledgments

This project began life in Oxford a number of years ago; acknowledgments are gratefully extended to those who gave me advice and suggestions at that time, especially professors Terry Eagleton, Christopher Butler, Bernard Richards, Kate Flint, Lyndall Gordon, Mike Dawney, and Judith Williamson.

A version of chapter 1 of this book was published as "Bakhtin and Popular Culture" in *New Literary History* 23.3 (1992); an earlier version of chapter 2 was published as "Joyful Mayhem: Bakhtin and Football Chants" in *Text and Performance Quarterly* 14.4 (1993); a section of chapter 3 was published as "Classical Trivia: The Rhetoric of Page 3" in *PostScript* 3 (1997); a section of chapter 4 was published as "The Last Stop of Desire: The Spatial Text of Covent Garden" in *Consumption, Markets and Culture* 1.1 (1996); a section of chapter 5 was published as "Blue Prints and Bodies" in the book *Ethics and the Subject*, ed. Karl Simms, Amsterdam: Rodopi Press, 1997. Thanks to all concerned for permissions to republish the aforementioned parts of the book.

Introduction: Popular Culture and Its Critics

The identity of any form of culture as an intellectual discipline has always been dependent for its existence on the Other that occupies the space outside the academic enclosure. This forbidden, taboo, and often degraded Other is all the language, writing, and art that is *not* generally classed as "culture," against which the "self" of culture "proper" is formed. In the last fifteen years, it has been consistently argued that any discipline that fails to take into account 90 percent or more of what constitutes its domain will not only have huge zones of blindness, but will also run serious risks of distorted vision in understanding the small zone it *does* focus on.

In the past fifteen years, it has become quite common for the reader of academic journals in the broad field of cultural studies to come across articles on post-structural linguistics side-by-side with thoughtful essays on soap opera, rock music, and Hollywood movies. At the same time, popular style magazines often contain clever reviews of literature, careful decodings of lyrics and images, and trenchant articles on phases in popular music, fashion, and advertising. In the academy, literature courses in many universities are proving less popular than (and sharing much ground with) the faculties of cultural studies. It is now commonly argued that, in the light of recent theories of postmodernism, *bricolage* and the collapse of various genre barriers, the high–low cultural divide need no longer be argued.

And yet much of the academic analysis directed at popular culture has been distinguished by a general uncertainty over which methods to use, confusion over the absence of any universally agreed basic theory or groundwork, and opposition from an academic canon suspicious of material so generally available. Forced into defensive positions by consistent justifications of the use of data that by definition seems too frivolous to warrant serious investigation—data that is often considered less important and significant than canonical texts and too banal, trivial, or unsuitable to constitute a part of the cultural tradition—academic defenders of popular culture have too frequently fallen into strategies that appear to concede a certain validity to the attacks of their detractors. These strategies include the general assumption that most forms of popular culture are not substantial enough to respond to the same complex intellectual treatment that is regularly applied to canonical cultural texts.

Academic interest in the historical stability of the canon began in the 1960s, when the French scholars Pierre Macherey and Etienne Balibar began to debate whether literary texts should be considered "literary" in themselves, according to their own intrinsic characteristics, which distinguish them from "nonliterary" texts. They concluded that a text is "literary" because it is recognized as such, at a certain moment, under certain conditions. The cultural or literary canon, argued Macherey and Balibar, must be regarded as an accidental and temporary historical construct rather than a fixed entity, and one that is constantly open to revision.

Indeed, as Macherey and Balibar suggest, the very concept of "the literary" is always based on a series of exclusions that themselves assume an idea of culture as concerned with certain "high," "universal" values that are not, in fact, static or independent, but random, ephemeral, and historically determinate. There will always be a cultural context in which the marginal is the mainstream, and vice versa. Moreover, the movement of any form of activity from cultural periphery to cultural center also involves a transformation in the very "essence" of that activity. So the "essence" of "high" or "literary" culture is in fact far from ahistorical; historicity invades the very nature of these modes of activity and their products. It is the fixity of the hierarchical scale of values, and the arbitrariness of its contents at any given point, which provide the scale with its particular power.

Moreover, of course, the very label itself, "popular culture," needs a fixed scale of differentiation in order to exist, since it is mostly defined in terms of what it is not—opera, theater, poetry, classical music, and so on. And yet it is well known that writers such as Samuel Richardson, Charles Dickens, Mark Twain, and James Fenimore Cooper have now been accorded "classic" status, despite their one-time popularity and their use of such "low" cultural tools as melodrama, scandal, burlesque, stereotype, and violent action. The "classic" status of these writers is now defended through reference to the familiar terms of literary criticism (structure, irony, tragic consciousness, and so on) and, ultimately, through their association with other "literary" figures and artifacts.

Popular culture, then, can apparently be transformed into "high" culture by a simple critical act of appropriation. Indeed, so insecure are these categories that the popular culture of one decade can easily become the high culture of the next—a fact that applies today not only to individual artists (Tom Wolfe, William Burroughs, Raymond Chandler, Jay McInerney, Bret Easton Ellis), but also to styles (romanticism, magic realism), and even genres (science fiction, horror).

This raises the significant issue of how the "popular" is then to be defined. Is it to be defined as a formal property of certain cultural goods? Do the texts themselves determine their readings, and hence define "popularity?" Is "popularity" related to who is doing the consuming? For the purposes of this book, in which the texts I analyze range from films, to style magazines, to the activities of shopping and sports supporting, I am defining popularity as dependent on not *who* is doing the consuming, but on *how many* are doing the consuming. Thus, for the purposes of this book, a text is part of popular culture if it fits in with a phase of general understanding, if it is familiar to the most widely shared manners and tastes prevalent in Western culture today, and if it effects and is ordinarily understood, shared and enjoyed by a large proportion of the general population.

Because of its wide levels of distribution, popular culture is normally associated with the instruments of the mass media (film, television, and journalism), usually has a commercial basis, and is produced as a commodity for the purposes of making money. There are, of course, a number of exceptions to this description: "high" cultural forms can often be commercially successful and attract mass audiences, like the music of Luciano Pavarotti, Enrico Caruso, and Yo-Yo Ma, and "popular" culture can be widely unpopular, like the much-criticized but widely viewed "reality" television shows.

The connection between popular culture, mass media, and capitalism means that most popular cultural texts tend to attract ideological or gender-based critiques, since such perspectives presumably offer the most immediate potential for understanding the appeal, circulation, and effects of popular cultural forms. Consequently, academic analysis of these texts generally considers them as a socially or historically valuable phenomenon, placing them in a sociohistorical context and approaching them in terms of the motives for their initial creation, looking at how and where they are read, watched, and enjoyed.

Today, most critics of popular culture defend the powers of cultural theory to appropriate a variety of texts for critical analysis, including certain social phenomena other than "academically respectable" cultural forms, so as to illustrate their meanings for individuals and their societies. Scholars tend to focus on the way in which social rules governing an aesthetic practice order its valuations or ideologies. The substance of the text is generally regarded as a consequence of its displacement or marginalization by something "else" that is external to it—by some other kind of social practice, such as politics, ideology, distribution, or effects. Genre analysis, for example, approaches popular texts in terms of other critical theories and institutions, such as formalism or structuralism, or post-formalism or post-structuralism, in terms, for example, of the works of Vladimir Propp, Tsvetan Toderov, or Michel Foucault.

In this introduction, I want to take a look at the various kinds of analysis that have been directed at popular culture from 1950 to the present day, suggesting how and in what ways my own analysis—the study of popular culture chiefly in terms of its own formations of pleasure—both relies upon, and differs from, this previous and current research. My own interest in popular culture principally involves an appreciation of the cultural objects themselves, and, in particular, of the pleasures they can yield. However, since a concept such as pleasure is a preeminently social notion, it is doubtful whether it can be wholly separated from the social and ideological determinants of the cultural texts themselves. Consequently, any analysis of popular cultural texts in their own terms, as specific processes of meaning and pleasure creation for the consumer, will necessarily at times rely heavily on ideological theory.

Conservative Criticism

The earliest critics of postwar popular culture were highly pessimistic about the detrimental moral effects they believed were a result of the growth of the mass media. It was felt that democratic access to popular fiction, for example, would inevitably lead to "useless knowledge," idleness, and cultural degeneration. The earliest critics of popular culture considered ex-canonical texts as worthy of study only so that a gullible public could be enlightened as to their faults and failings, their "unsuitable" elements of subject matter or style. This tradition of pessimistic critique emerged in the 1950s with Bernard Rosenberg's and David M. White's *Mass Culture—The Popular Arts in America* (1957). In "Avant-Garde and Kitsch," this volume's most widely quoted essay, cultural critic Clement Greenberg suggests that the problem with contemporary popular culture is that it appropriates debased simulacra and inauthentic imitations of "high" culture for its raw materials. He argues that popular culture welcomes and cultivates "insensibility," that it is "mechanical" and operates by formulas, and that it presents "vicarious experience and faked sensations" (102). Greenberg believed that popular culture provides a kind of synthetic shortcut or detour to providing spurious, vicarious experience for the lazy consumer. This notion of "predigested culture" might today be quite appropriately applied to the vocabulary of popular style magazines, which I examine in chapter 1, which regularly and sometimes randomly play with a "high cultural" vocabulary—terms like "metatextual," "Foucauldian," and "postmodern."

Five years later, in *The Gutenberg Galaxy*—his famous 1962 discussion of advertising—cultural critic Marshall McLuhan suggested that the larger business monopolies are often drawn toward sponsorship of "the arts" by presenting their product in conjunction with "some aroma of the old masters of paint, pen or music" (41). In other words, according to McLuhan, by including a Brahms or Beethoven soundtrack to a television show or advertisement, "low" culture was attempting, through its financial power, to purchase some kind of sophisticated credibility by associating itself with the tools and products of another, "higher" level of culture. Similar arguments are sometimes used today in relation to the highly criticized union of art and advertising. For example, Oxford literature professor Bernard Richards considers "blasphemous" the use of the chorus of the Israelites from Verdi's *Nabucco* in an advertisement for British Airways, a Fison's soap ad that uses Blake's "Jerusalem" and the Parry setting, and the "mocking" of the Lady of the Lake in a beer commercial.

The conservative critics of the 1950s (Clement Greenberg, Ortega y Gasset, T. S. Eliot, Ernst van den Haag, and Q. D. Leavis) all seemed to agree that democracy was in some way or other "responsible" for popular culture, which was a regrettable part of the high price that had to be paid for the benefits of a democratic system. Gasset, Eliot, van den Haag, and Greenberg all believed that popular culture and the avant-garde aesthetic tradition were totally dissimilar, and any contact between them would simply endanger the latter. They believed popular culture to be a negative and detrimental side-effect of democracy, not necessarily because of its inappropriately "sub-literary" qualities, but because it might actually have a morally damaging effect on the consumer. It was widely believed that subjection to the influence of pulp novels, advertising, television, film, comic books, and magazines would inevitably have a harmful effect on the reader or audience. For example, in his essay "Boys' Weeklies" published in *Horizon* in 1939, George Orwell, referred to comic books as "pernicious rubbish" that "have almost no aesthetic interest" (27). Orwell believed that popular culture would continue to exert an evil influence over its audience so long as the mass media were considered as "private entertainments, with negligible effects on those who enjoy them, and with none whatsoever on those who pass them by" (27). Similarly, in her 1965 essay "Fiction and the Reading Public," Q. D. Leavis asserted that, for the reader who spends his (*sic*) leisure time indulging in the distractions offered by popular culture, "looking through magazines and newspapers and listening to jazz music does not merely fail to help him, it prevents him from normal development" (104).

By the 1970s and 1980s, it was no longer common for critics to regard popular culture as a cheap, trivial version of "high" culture, nor to equate "high" culture with lofty, humane thoughts and benevolent government. Nevertheless, conservative detractors of popular culture continued to make a case for its morally detrimental effects. Most of these critics argued quite substantially against what they believed to be the depersonalization, lack of control, and manipulative potential demonstrated by the mass media. They suggested that technology had become so pervasive that unrelenting efficiency was starting to dominate all dimensions of human life, thereby draining it of the richness and variety of earlier human cultures.

For example, Daniel Bell's *The Cultural Contradictions of Capitalism* (1976), Dwight Macdonald's *Against the American Grain: Essays on the Effects of Mass Culture* (1983), Allan Bloom's *The Closing of the American Mind* (1987), and E. D. Hirsch's *Cultural Literacy: What Every American Needs to Know* (1987) all convincingly argued that mass education and mass culture were to blame for decaying American standards of education. Similarly, Marie Winn's *The Plug-In Drug* (1975) and Jerry Mander's *Four Arguments for the Elimination of Television* (1978) both credibly blamed television for the breakdown of the family. Neil Postman's *Amusing Ourselves to Death* (1986) and Joshua Meyrowitz's *No Sense of Place* (1986) continued and extended Winn and Mander's arguments by explaining how childhood had been broken out of its isolation by television, a medium that requires no literacy for access, and which exposes one and all to adult as well as adolescent concerns. Further thoughtfully pessimistic critiques came from Christopher Lasch in *The Culture of Narcissism* (1978), and Noam Chomsky in *Towards a New Cold War* (1982).

In the last fifteen years, conservative critics of popular culture like Tom Schachtman and Herbert Schiller have begun to make the case that public consciousness has been colonized by corporate interests, leading to a breakdown in the democratic system, the absence of individual self-expression, and widescale inarticulacy and public boredom. This, according to critics like Schachtman and Schiller, is the cumulative result of fifty years of mass culture that has penetrated the private realm in the forms of television, advertising, cinema, VHS, DVD, and the Internet. The most devastating recent attacks on contemporary popular culture are to be found in Tom Schachtman's *Inarticulate Society: Eloquence and Culture in America* (1995), Herbert Schiller's *Culture, Inc.—The Corporate Takeover of Public Expression* (1991), and, more recently, Stuart Ewan's attack on media culture, *Captains of Consciousness* (2001).

In any discussion of the place of popular culture—particularly in any analysis of the pleasures such popular texts can yield—ideological criteria are clearly important. Against the more staunchly conservative detractors of popular culture, however, I would argue first that the reading public today, far from disintegrating under the influence of mechanization and an industrialized democratic society, has blossomed, and public reading tastes have become far more discriminating and diversified. Second, the argument that popular culture is inferior to and less important than "high" culture because it fails to use "high" culture's tools and traditions is obviously unstable, since these tools and traditions clearly become inapplicable at other times, and in other contexts. Of course, some elements of pop culture appear as substantial as traditional culture when measured by traditional standards; other elements, however, prove equally valuable only by essentially different, perhaps incommensurable standards.

Instead of getting tied down by value judgments that involve moral or ideological components, I want to think in this book about pop culture as an important source of aesthetic pleasure. This is an essentially hedonistic position, which clearly involves a number of philosophical issues. How, for example, is it possible to measure the *value* of the kinds of pleasure such texts produce? What if textual pleasure for one element of the audience is attained only at the expense of possible discomfort, suffering, and even perhaps even physical danger for others, as—some have argued—is the case with horror movies or pornography? What if the pleasures obtained from popular culture are of a morally or ethically dubious nature? What if this pleasure is used to deliberately conceal social, sexual, or political inequities, as in the case of the tabloid newspaper? How is it possible to guarantee that pop culture is used to give the kind of pleasure its originators intended, rather than to create disturbance and discomfort? It is these and related issues that guide my thoughts throughout this book.

Marxist Criticism

Ironically, the association made by many conservative critics between pop culture and democracy has, in its most extreme forms, a number of similarities with the dystopian, left-leaning accounts of pop culture expounded by the political philosophers of the Frankfurt School (Theodore Adorno, Max Horkheimer, Herbert Marcuse, Antonio Gramsci, and Walter Benjamin), and more subtly in the writings of Raymond Williams and Terry Eagleton. Although the political perspectives of this varied group diverge to such an extent that it is perhaps unwise to treat their strands of argument as undifferentiated, many of these philosophers would follow Alan Swingewood in arguing that popular culture developed out of the repression of the working classes, who were, according to Swingewood in *The Myth of Mass Culture* (1977), "deprived of any meaningful institutional access to bourgeois culture" (98). With the decline of Chartism and the independent radical press, argues Swingewood, "the working class reader had *no other alternative* than that of the new commercialized popular culture . . ." (99) (italics mine).

There has always been plenty of potential for the application of Marxist analysis to current manifestations of pop culture, mainly because this kind of culture is generally associated with the social forces essential to its creation—namely, urbanization and industrialization. By undermining the unique, hand-crafted quality of a work of art, the mechanics of mass production shattered the idea of a "tradition" built on a chain of autonomous artifacts, and the very concept of "traditional culture" itself became somewhat obsolete. More specifically, Frankfurt School theorists Theodore Adorno and Herbert Marcuse regarded the "irrelevant satisfactions" of popular culture as the instruments of repression. Adorno and Marcuse interpreted capitalist culture and its artifacts as commodities, their function to entertain, divert, and reduce consciousness to a state of total passivity. Other Marxist critics have interpreted popular cultural artifacts such as magazines, comic books, and tabloid journalism, for example, as purposely "reconciling" the listener, reader, or audience to the dominant ideology or status quo, and making their role one of absolute passivity. Adorno, for example, in his famous essay "The Culture Industry" (1972), interprets culture as intentionally "integrating" its consumers from above, and through an ideology in which "conformity has replaced consciousness" (18).

Adorno's arguments are shared by Walter Benjamin, who believes that when people are organized into masses, they lose their human identity and quality, and fail to relate to one another at all except as part of the repressed crowd—something distant, abstract, and inhuman, connected in some way to the "deterministic" influence of technology. The links made by Benjamin in *Illuminations* (1969) between the mass organization of capitalist society and the loss of human identity may have some pressing connection with what he considered to be the anaesthetic effects of pop culture as an anodyne to the repressive trends of capitalism.

On the other hand, there are a number of Marxist critics who believe pop culture to be more substantial and necessary than traditional culture. This, they argue, is because it has a wider, larger, and socially broader audience than those who attend operas, art exhibitions, and the ballet, and because it usually depends for its creation on collaborative teams of paid actors, script-writers, journalists, managers and musicians, and so on. According to some left-leaning critics, this helpfully contradicts the general assumption that individual cultural creativity is necessarily different from and "better than" collaborative cultural production.

Other leftist critics have argued that pop culture represents the development of strong, working-class political and social institutions within the framework of a mature capitalist social formation. This, they argue, implies that the real democratization of culture which has occurred within modern capitalism has functioned to undermine traditional bases of cultural value and "legitimacy" and replace them with the secular values of the masses. As Alan Swingewood writes, "the decay of the 'high cultured aura,' the mass reproduction of high culture and recent trends toward the artistic depiction of reality in everyday terms are elements of a *potentially democratic culture*, and not the symptoms of cultural stagnation or decline" (99).

Different strands of Marxist argument continued into the 1980s and 1990s, with publications like Terry Eagleton's *The Function of Criticism* (1984), George McCarthy's *Dialectics and Decadance* (1994), John McCracken's *Rencontres* (2000), and Graeme Turner's *British Cultural Studies* (1996). In the last ten years, the most influential leftist critic of mass culture has without a doubt been Noam Chomsky, whose critiques of the media are among the most powerful writings on the subject, especially his book *Media Control—The Spectacular Achievements of Propaganda* (2002). Other important leftist works on the influence of popular culture in the past ten years include Frederic Jameson and Masao Miyoshi's writing on globalism, Jean Baudrillard's studies of postmodern American culture, and Umberto Eco's recent work in semiotics, particularly *Interpretation and Overinterpretation* (1992). Especially interesting is the work of Steven Best and Douglas Kellner on the inter-relation of science, the media, technology, and cultural studies. *The Postmodern Turn* (1997) considers the relationship of postmodernity to modernity in the arts, science, politics, and theory, and *The Postmodern Adventure* (2001) examines the interface of science, technology, and cultural studies at the beginning of the third millenium.

There have always been a significant number of observers of popular culture, not necessarily Marxists themselves, who tend to share the Marxist principle that popular culture is one of the many detrimental side-effects of a dystopian society, the crude yet inevitable result of the repressions of consumer capitalism, an antirevolutionary narcotic. In his 1972 essay "Mass Culture or Democratization of Culture?"—a work more sympathetic than his earlier criticism—Dwight Macdonald described popular culture as a culture fabricated by technicians hired by businessmen whose audience are passive consumers, their choice limited between buying and not buying (94). In this essay, Macdonald argued that mass culture reinforces those attitudes—such as passivity and boredom—that seem inseparable from existence in modern society, thus treating popular culture as the object of neo-Puritan reprobation common to much Marxist-influenced cultural critique. Similarly, Clement Greenberg in the 1950s suggested that the avant-garde of that time depended for its audience on "the rich and the cultivated," who were becoming more and more timid in the face of the mass media and the popularity of kitsch—something Greenberg identified as a com-mercial and profit-making result of the Industrial Revolution and mass literacy.

Critics who associated pop culture with the detrimental side-effects of capitalism generally described this kind of culture as being constructed around the mechanical representation of cultural objects. For example, in *The Making of the English Working Classes* (1966), critic E. P. Thomson regarded capitalism as responsible for the rise of mass culture, claiming that such culture was not necessarily what the public *desired*, but what it had been brainwashed into *wanting* by the capitalist tools of television and advertising. Artist Richard Hamilton made a similar argument (1983). "As monopolistic tendencies increase," wrote Hamilton, "we can expect a more systematic application of control tech-niques with greater power to instil the craving to consume" (17). Hamilton seemed to be implying that subjectivity was a passive state to be worked upon by the powers of commodity fetishism, rather than being itself formed through the entry into language and culture.

Such arguments, although essentially subjective, have a certain unde-niable validity. For example, it is impossible to deny the fundamental connections between pop culture and capitalism, even though pop culture flourishes wherever the appropriate technological apparatus exists, even in noncapitalist societies such as the former Soviet Union. However, it is not necessarily the lower socioeconomic groups that demand and consume popular culture, a fact that has been ratified by numerous surveys revealing cross-class consumption figures for maga-zines, tabloids, and comic books, and demographically diverse viewing figures for soap operas, chat shows, film, and popular fiction. These figures suggest that the relationship between pop culture and capitalism has always been, and remains, manifestly dynamic and contradictory.

Historical Criticism

There is also a very long tradition of social historical work on cultural formations, going back to de Tocqueville and beyond. Since the 1970s, a lot of important work has been undertaken on the history of popu-lar cultural forms and their role within modern society. In their book *Literacy in Traditional Societies* (1989), historians Jack Goody and Ian Watt have shown, for example, that during the course of the eigh-teenth century, the democratizing of culture that was set in motion by cheap printing, libraries, newspapers, and the middle-class reading public excluded the working classes on both an economic and a literary basis. Goody and Watt criticize versions of mass culture theory based on the myth of a "golden organic past" which tend, they claim, to ignore standards of literacy. They suggest that in earlier societies, oral culture was dominated by traditionalistic elements that make analytic readings impossible, and it is only with the development of writing and the intellectual skills associated with it that it becomes possible to formally separate the various elements of culture, and thus allow for critical evaluation.

The best historical studies of popular culture are those that attempt to trace the techniques employed by contemporary pop cultural forms back to the traditions of the nineteenth-century novel, early comic books, magazine illustrations, popular literature, and the entertainments of the theater, music hall, fairground, and parlor. Popular narrative traditions in cinema and television, for example, have been linked back to the growth of reading habits, copyright agreements, banking inter-ests, publication, the history of magazine serialization, the way in which cities started to dominate cultural life in new and unsuspected ways, and how standardization and syndication were an inevitable response to the realities of the contemporary economic climate. For instance, John L. Fell in *Film in the Narrative Tradition* (1986) argues that in motion pictures, there surfaced an entire tradition of narrative technique that had been developing unsystematically for over a hundred years, and which appeared sporadically in ephemera as diverse as stereograph sets, zoetropes, peep shows, song slides, and postcards. Similarly, Richard Maltby's *Dreams for Sale* (1989) studies the history of consumption in film, pop music, design, fashion, media, and sport—those elements of pop culture that are consumed most avidly. Maltby lays emphasis on consumption rather than production in order to analyze the way in which objects are bought, sold, used, and thrown away. He shows how an understanding of this process explains the role of consumer items more clearly than would a simple record of their production.

The historical implications of pop culture obviously play a significant part in any analysis of popular texts. Interesting as such implications are, however, this historical approach at first seems unsuitable. Cycles in trade names and advertising, for example, have virtually no historical memory. Recycled trademarks and retro styles appear to be greeted as innovations. Discussions of advertising, particularly in American national life, often lack a historical dimension, and consequently, much historical analysis of popular cultural texts seems at first inappropriate. Further, the very application of historically proven "universal" moral and aesthetic standards seems to have little relevance to the ephemeral, disposable culture of the masses. As historian Reyner Banham writes in his book *Theory and Design in the First Machine Age* (1980):

> We easily consume noisy ephemeridae, here with a bang today, gone without a whimper tomorrow—movies, beachwear, pulp magazines, this morning's headlines and tomorrow's television programmes—yet we insist on aesthetic and moral standards hitched to permanency, durability, perennity. (7)

On the other hand, of course, nothing is completely ahistorical, and one might argue that especially *commercial* culture's appearance of having no past is deceptive, and all part of the illusion of newness and futurity that modern consumer culture tries to generate. To see consumer culture as ahistorical could be interpreted as buying into the illusion—and also the ideology underpinning the illusion—of consumer capitalism.

Feminist Criticism

Much of the most interesting and important work on pop culture that has been produced since the 1960s has been inflected by a feminist position. Not only are feminist critics paying increasing attention to pop culture as a valuable source of cultural analysis and information, but there is also a major interest in such work in departments of literary studies and English. Important developments in British feminist analysis of popular cultural forms began with the publication of Angela McRobbie's 1978 study of the girls' magazine *Jackie* in terms of the ideology of adolescent femininity, which has been followed up by Linda Christian-Smith's work on adolescent romance novels and the construction of the feminine (1987, 1988, 1990). In the United States, principal figures in this field include Janice Radway, whose *Reading the Romance*, a study of the status of women's romantic fiction as a highly sophisticated form of the original prototypical category literature, was published in 1987. Radway has since gone on to study the Book-of-the-Month club, and the role played by women in reading groups.

One of the most helpful and intriguing conclusions reached by Radway, as well as by other feminist critics like Meaghan Morris, is that the text comes alive and communicates only when its viewers provide it with their own interpretations and understandings. This is a conclusion reached by feminist critics working on media and television audiences, most notably Ien Ang in her work on *Dallas* (1985). My own interest in pop culture shares much ground with Tania Modelski's feminist reception theory, as well as other feminist writing on pop culture, especially the work of Laura Kipnis, Emily Martin, and Elspeth Probyn.

Most feminist writing on popular culture is useful in the way it emphasizes the interaction of the textual with the extra-textual, and the way it combines analysis of the formal properties of the text with involvement in ideological issues, which might also play an important role in the consumer's response. Feminist theory, in fact, has an integral part in further investigating some of the philosophical problems espoused by any sympathetic examination of pop culture as a source of aesthetic pleasure, especially the difficulties attendant on my own hedonistic approach.

Unlike my own work, however, most feminist theory does not encourage a sympathetic "relaxed comfortableness" about the role of popular culture in society. It generally tends to ignore the fallacy that popular culture is too shifting, trivial, or transient to have any kind of lasting effect—a fallacy that is frequently considered to defeat even the need for criticism. Feminist theory also refuses to allow the morally neutral methodological stance of "objective science" to be translated into an excuse to avoid judgment. From a feminist perspective, what are often seen as morally dubious instances of popular culture (such as potentially degrading images of sex and violence) will never be merely measured—as though, as some social science research might have us believe, anything that exists is acceptable and worth studying—but analyzed instead in terms of their role in society, their presentation of gender, their association with other media images and stereotypes, their effect on their audience and their possibly harmful effects on the consumer.

The Scholar-Fans

The role of popular culture today seems to be changing faster and faster as it is becoming an increasingly respectable field of academic interest, and as the field of cultural studies seems to be widening to include more and more diverse and formerly ex-canonical texts. Critics working in the field of cultural studies generally espouse a liberal approach to the aesthetics of popular culture, and the establishment of cultural studies departments over the last two decades has made it quite acceptable for academics not only to study popular culture, but also to admit that they like it and enjoy it. This has created the recent phenomenon of the scholar-fan, whose affection for his or her subject can be quite passionate (see, e.g., the work of Martin Barker [1984] on horror comics, or Meaghan Morris [1997] on shopping).

However, a heavy dose of such writing can create a sense of overly unquestioning sympathy toward pop culture. Examples of this tendency include Christopher D. Geist's *The Popular Culture Reader* (1983), Steve Redhead's *The End of the Century Party* (1990), and especially articles published in *The Journal of Popular Culture*, *The Journal of American Culture*, and other works from Bowling Green State University Popular Press. The discipline of cultural studies can, at its worst, weld together a mismatch of varying perspectives (ethnographic, feminist, sociological, psychoanalytic, and so on), which occasionally produces confusing readings, many of which suffer from an overload of ideology, which detracts from the role of popular culture as a source of aesthetic pleasure. And yet, in the end, it is essentially impossible to escape from moral and ideological criteria in any examination of popular cultural texts—partly because pleasure is an ideological phenomenon anyway, and partly because much of the pleasure produced by such texts emerges from the presentation of radical and often unpopular views addressing social, political, racial and sexual inequities, and so on, thereby expressing explicit versions of normally repressed ideas about the status quo.

Postmodernism and Popular Culture

One of the hallmarks of many recent cultural theories is that they recognize the appeal and delight generated by popular cultural artifacts with minimal aesthetic or cultural prejudice, appreciating that pop culture can be a unique and substantial means of pleasure-creation in its own right. It could perhaps be argued, however, that such theories never quite succeed in appropriately utilizing pop cultural artifacts because of the rather uncertain relationship between high theory and low culture. Many critics would suggest that, in the last twenty years, distinctions between direct culture itself and indirect *commentary* upon that culture have become blurred. Theorists such as David Carroll in *Paraesthetics* (1989) and Patrick Brantlinger in *Crusoe's Footprints* (1990) have suggested that the popularity and accessibility of postmodern styles and ideas may simply be manifestations of another "high" cultural attitude, stance, or style. On the other hand, Lawrence Alloway in *Modern Dreams* (1987) and Dick Hebdige in *Hiding in the Light* (1988) have both suggested that postmodernism should not be regarded as a *style*, but rather as something that implicitly *challenges* the notion of style.

Hebdige's interpretation of postmodernism is of a cultural category with a conceptual basis that implicitly questions the relationship between popular culture and aesthetics, presents art as critique, and challenges the relations between the aesthetic, the political, and the undetermined ends of theory and art. Hebdige argues that postmodern culture is based not on intellectual or theoretical abstraction, but on the rediscovery of a culture's connection to the concrete, the fusion of text and performance, the merging of the textual and the lived. Due to this conceptual basis, postmodern culture tends to use popular artifacts quite directly, in order to draw attention to the very question of culture, avoiding comment, or blurring the boundaries between presentation and comment. For example, the work of Andy Warhol suggests that neither the artist nor the artifact should be taken too seriously. In Warhol, according to cultural commentator Lawrence Alloway (1988), "no interpretation is offered save the tacit irony resulting from a deadpan presentation of the banal in the context of artistic seriousness. Context becomes content" (96). This kind of art thereby undermines the concept of "high" culture by suggesting that popular and "high" culture are virtually interchangeable—or at least, the distinction between them is blurred.

Alloway argues that much of postmodernism tackles the question of how traditions come about, how things come to be traditional—that is, inherited, rather than discovered or invented. He suggests that the stimulus behind postmodern culture is a drive to replace culture as an object of contemplation with culture as a system of communication. By appropriating and utilizing popular forms, therefore, postmodern culture can effectively problematize the terms in which culture is discussed by abandoning the tone of solemnity and seriousness usually appropriate to "radical" bourgeois culture and cultural criticism. By so doing, postmodern cultural artifacts draw our attention to the complicity between aesthetic taste, and economic and symbolic power.

As a result, Alloway suggests, postmodern culture regularly and happily incorporates many of the characteristics of popular culture, often in the context of play, parody, or pastiche. Postmodern culture is often based, for example, on formulas that consist of standardized practices for creating aesthetic effects, new versions of which can rapidly be mass-produced. Andy Warhol's themes, techniques, materials, and images, which all drew on popular culture—his studio itself was called "the Factory"—have paved the way in the twenty-first century for silkscreen prints, "designer" pop hits, faux preowned jeans, and self-reflexive ad campaigns.

These kinds of postmodern cultural artifacts, as Alloway suggests, tend to obliterate differences between the popular and the commercial, eliminating traditional distinctions between the consumer-based, money-making designs of mass capitalist culture and autonomous, noncommercial artifacts. Postmodernism therefore shares capitalism's obsessions—with appearance, with seeming rather than being, gesture rather than substance and the process of the transaction itself—as an implicit commentary on the impact of media culture as a form of modern life.

Formations of Pleasure

My own interest in pop culture has led me to understand various types of cultural product in terms of a kind of "cultural pluralism," a sort of dynamic, horizontal structure rather than the current "pyramid hierarchy" of cultural forms. I take this approach because I am interested in the vast range of social groups and networks that contemporary pop culture contains, each with its own distinctive style and set of formations. However, resistant subcultures or countercultures may themselves often develop into new forms of traditional culture by revising the meanings attached to existing cultural forms. As I explain in chapter 1, for example, punk—originally a marginal subculture— altered the conventional meanings of a wide range of commercial phenomena, including fashion, music, and art, in order to express an ideology of alienation and a rejection of traditional cultural values. The aesthetic discoveries of the avant-garde, in fact, are often derived from a selective appropriation of the fringe popular culture as developed by nonelite groups such as advertisers and manufacturers.

The forms of pop culture I consider in this book have been selected primarily for aesthetic reasons—they are all full of irony; they are all profanely productive and deathless creations; they are all infected with the spirit of process and inconclusiveness, thereby breaking up the otherwise grim atmosphere of traditional society. They all possess a ludicrous and carnivalesque creativity and vitality far from fatalism and pessimism, and it is this basic centripetal force that gives them such power. Punk, style magazines, tabloid newspapers, pornography, football, shopping, and horror fictions are all present, *active* forms associated with folk traditions, affirming a lack of distance between the real and the textual. Indeed, the basis of the identity of most forms of pop culture is the commonplace and obvious nature of the physical and social world.

In this book, I consider the possibilities offered by the work of three twentieth-century critical theorists—Mikhail M. Bakhtin, Roland Barthes, and Jacques Lacan—for an appreciation of contemporary popular culture according to the codes and formations by which it produces pleasure. Each of these theorists concentrates on a highly different aspect of culture—Bakhtin the dialogic, Barthes the semiotic, and Lacan the psychoanalytic. All three theorists also provide radical interpretations of canon and genre that allow for an approach to genre-study that implies an open-mindedness and an open-endedness. Moreover, these three theorists cover, historically, much of the twentieth century, from Bakhtin's *Problems of Dostoyevsky's Poetics*, first published in 1929, to Barthes's *Mythologies*, first published in 1988. Bakhtin, Barthes, and Lacan have all contributed to the opening up of a theoretical space for a series of liberal readings of popular culture, whose ultimate possibilities we cannot foresee. These three names recur again and again whenever the nature of popular culture is taken into question. They all, in different ways, rethink the concepts of style and genre in the light of a Saussurean or post-Saussurean linguistics.

In this book, my own analysis of popular culture develops from the work of these key thinkers. In the chapters that follow, I demonstrate different ways of elucidating particular theoretical elements and emerging directions in pop culture by considering various of its forms so as to understand how and why it is so popular, and how it creates so much pleasure on the part of the consumer. I have tried to select forms of popular culture that are intended to generate enjoyment for the consumer or participant, while providing a wide range of cultural contexts, from the written (tabloid newspapers, style magazines), to the visual (pornography and horror films), to the activities of sports fandom and shopping. These forms all involve a familiarity with the omnipresent images of capitalism and consumption, and they all, if not consciously, celebrate the transactions that take place at home, in the street, in the movie theater, or in front of the television; the delights of conspicuous consumption; the quality of temporariness and the strategies of bodily life.

One issue that might be raised at this point is why this sort of textual analysis is particularly appropriate to *popular* culture, and if these pleasures are the pleasures that *all* readers get from these fictions and representations, whether they know it or not. On the first point, I would argue that there are a lot of ways in which these particular theoretical directions are particularly apposite to popular cultural texts—indeed, Barthes and Bakhtin especially both have a lot to say about popular culture, and its role in society. Nevertheless, I am not suggesting that the work of Lacan offers the definitive reading of pornography, that Barthes provides the best potential for an analysis of tabloid newspapers, and so on. In fact, each type of popular culture that I investigate here may well benefit from a variety of readings, and, indeed, from a whole range of theoretical approaches. My investigation concludes that there is a range of different kinds and qualities of pleasure to be gained from pop culture, and the type of pleasure attained depends to a great extent on the way the text is being consumed, the relation between spectator and subject, and the relation between subjectivity and issues like age, gender, and social class. And yet it does seem to be true that certain critical theories provide a wider scope for understanding the consumer's pleasure. Perhaps the appropriation of a *bricolage* of the most apposite theoretical perspectives fits neatly with recent ideas about postmodern culture and the collapse of genre barriers. Whatever the theoretical perspective employed, however, any thoughtful analysis of pop culture will show that, contrary to popular belief, its fictions and representations respond surprisingly well to complex intellectual treatment, and in fact, for the most part, are a lot more substantial and interesting than has generally been assumed.

CHAPTER 1

CARNIVAL AND CHRONOTOPE: BAKHTIN AND STYLE MAGAZINES

Mikhail M. Bakhtin is gradually emerging as one of the leading theorists of the twentieth century, not only in literary circles, but wherever the fundamental nature of "literature" and "culture" is taken into question. Despite the checkered history of his own writing career and the impossible confusion of manuscripts and authorization,[1] Bakhtin is perhaps the most important and certainly the most radical writer of recent years to wholly rethink the concepts of style and genre in the light of a post-Saussurean linguistics.

However, Bakhtin attacked those linguists, including Saussure, who treated language as a dead, neutral, and static object of investigation. He viewed verbal signs as the arena of continuous class struggles. The ruling class, believed Bakhtin, generally try to narrow the meaning of words, and to make social signs uni-accentual, but the vitality and basic multi-accentuality of linguistic signs always becomes apparent as various class interests clash and intersect. According to Bakhtin, discourse can never be simple and holistic, but instead must be split into a series of interacting metalanguages, sometimes conflicting, sometimes at play. This interaction between a series of fundamental discourses recurs, claims Bakhtin, at every level of conversation, within whatever context the utterance is made. He described this interaction as *polyglossia*, referring to the basic condition governing the production of meaning in all discourses. Polyglossia asserts the way in which *context* defines the meaning of utterances, which are polyglot in so far as they put into play a multiplicity of social voices and their individual expressions. A single voice may give the impression of unity and closure, but the utterance is constantly (and to some extent unconsciously) producing a plenitude of meanings, which themselves stem from social interaction.

This polyglossia, according to Bakthin, is most radical and significant at times of festivity or social unrest, especially in the time he refers to as *carnival*, a phenomenon that has important applications both to particular texts, and to the history of literary genres. The festivities associated with carnival are collective and popular; the sacred is profaned, and the relativity of all things is proclaimed. At the time of carnival, everything authoritative, rigid, or serious is subverted, loosened, and mocked. Aberrant layers of history and culture come to replace or intrude upon more conventional cultural models, creatively transforming both language and culture into a vast, multi-layered dialogue. This essentially popular and libertarian social phenomenon has an important formative influence on the literature of different periods, the earliest carnivalized forms, according to Bakhtin, being the Socratic dialogue and the Menippean satire.

In *Problems of Dostoyevskys Poetics* (1929), Bakhtin developed a bold contrast between the modes of Tolstoy and those of Dostoyevsky. In the former, he claims, the various voices we hear are strictly subordinated to the author's controlling purpose. There is only one truth—the author's. In contrast to this monologic type of novel, according to Bakhtin, Dostoyevsky developed a new polyphonic (or *dialogic*) form, in which no attempt is made to orchestrate or unify the various points of view expressed by the different characters. The consciousnesses of the novel's characters do not merge with that of the author, nor do they become subordinated to the author's viewpoint, but they retain an integrity and independence; they are not only objects of the author's word, but subjects of their own universe. In *Rabelais and His World* (1968), Bakhtin explores the liberating and often subversive use of various dialogue forms in classical, medieval, and renaissance cultures.

Both of these works are highly relevant to my focus in the following two chapters. However, the primary text most relevant to my case is Bakhtin's "Discourse in the Novel," published in *The Dialogic Imagination* and written in 1938. I tend to focus primarily on this essay and other chapters from this work, particularly "Epic and Novel" (EN), and "Forms of Time and Chronotope in the Novel" (FT), rather than the earlier texts, since it is in these later essays that Bakhtin begins to reconsider the innate structure of the novel. Indeed, Bakhtin and the Bakhtin School opened up this genre to include a wide variety of different types of what Bakhtin referred to as *novelization*, basically deconstructing the novelistic canon until it embraces vastly differing branches of what was previously ex-canonical discourse. Bakhtin himself admitted that his reinterpretation of novelization possessed a finite set of organizing principles, only they were principles very different from those that had been previously considered.

There are currently a number of contemporary critics writing substantially on Bakhtin, including Graham Pechey, Ken Hirschkop, David Shepherd, and David Patterson. Pechey (1998) has analyzed the ways in which Bakhtin was influenced by Marxism in his belief that language cannot be separated from an intimate connection with ideology, drawing literature into the social and economic sphere, suggesting that language, a socially constructed system, is itself a material reality. Hirschkop and Shepherd (1989) have looked at some of Bakhtin's ideas in relation to cultural theory, paying particular attention to his concern with discourse as a social and cultural phenomenon, a system of active, dynamic social signs, capable of taking on different meanings and connotations for different social classes in various social, cultural, and historical situations. David Patterson (1985) has suggested that Bakhtin's emphasis on the spirit of carnival breaks up the formerly unquestioned organicism of the literary text and promotes the idea that major literary works may be multileveled and resistant to unification, showing how Bakhtin forms a basis for cultural criticism based on liberty and pleasure, rather than authority and decorum.

Bakhtin and Popular Culture

Bakhtin is acknowledged in increasingly wide circles as a sensitive observer of popular culture in its sociohistoric context. His acute study of the folkloric rituals of carnival—from the phallophors of epic Saturnalia, whose role was to joke and cavort obscenely, to the rogue comedians at turn-of-the-century country fair—uncovers a vast and fertile dialogue of polyglossia.[2] Not only at the carnival but pervading all levels of language, Bakhtin identifies infinitely shifting polyglottal strata made up of loosely bound generic wholes, accents, systems, and dialects, at battle, or at play. This dialogic scheme covers, in *The Dialogic Imagination* (DI) and *Rabelais and His World* (RW), most epic drama and Russian and European nineteenth-century realist literature, and invites its own extension into areas of recent popular culture.

Although Bakhtin insists that the novel is the key form of the time, his advantage over everyone else working on novel theory is his appreciation that the novel, rather than assimilating its language to form, shapes its form to languages, and consequently appears as what Michael Holquist describes as a "supergenre," ingesting and engulfing all other genres. Therefore the range of texts composed of a series of different languages interpenetrating one another—Bakhtin's classification of "novelness"—must clearly be immense. In fact, rather than limiting the term *novel* to a narrow definition of a piece of textual fiction, Bakhtin uses it to name the interplay of polyglottal strata at work within any given literary system in order to reveal the artificial limits and constrains of that system; for novelization as Bakhtin sees it is fundamentally opposed to the ordering into genres and canons that is characteristic of most literary discourse.

Bakhtin's version of novelization does not permit generic monologue, but rather insists on an interplay of dialogues between what any given system admits as literature, or high culture, or art, and, on the other hand, all those texts excluded from these definitions as nonliterature, low culture, popular culture, or subculture. *All* writing features this interplay, and therefore *all* kinds of language, even those which might not be classed as higher literary forms by the traditional critic represent, to Bakhtin, important forms of novelization. That piece of textual fiction more conventionally described as the novel is merely the most refined and distilled version of this definition, which spills over into other kinds of texts and novels in other times. As Bakhtin himself writes in "Discourse in the Novel," texts continue to grow and develop even after the moment of their creation, and they are capable of being creatively transformed in different eras, far distant from the day and hour of their original birth (422).

Bakhtinan analysis constitutes, then, a theoretical system to which it is not only possible but critically essential to submit today's popular culture, since in its continual interchange and deliberate fusion of high and low styles, politics, parody and pastiche, comic strip and literature, *haut couture* and street fashion, this kind of culture constitutes a singular shifting polyglossia whose rich carnival of discourse lies open to Bakhtin's radical definition of novelness, and whose instances of language, say in rock lyrics or advertisements, are in this way very similar to the instances of language that Bakhtin finds in the novel.

It is vital, however, to realize that, according to Bakhtin, in any analysis of the social ideology of genres such as high and low styles, politics, parody, or pastiche, it is impossible to escape the fact that the author/artist/designer is Russian or Polish, Jewish or Catholic, male or female, old or young, formally educated or formally uneducated, and so on. Bakhtin finds it difficult to identify specific genres beyond relatively stable *forms of construction of the whole* in every discourse and utterance, from the literary and the rhetorical to the spontaneous and the everyday—hence his theory of sociopolitical genre, or generic wholes. Real genres as such do not actually *exist*; rather, they *play* at being all-encompassing and total. Consequently, the very notion of a unity is false, since that supposed unity encompasses infinite strata of other, autonomous unities. Absolute, ideal extremes are illusory; it is possible to theorize and quantify only, according to Bakhtin, in terms of approximate wholes and the generalization of generic regularities.

Bakhtin's theory of polyglossia rests upon his vision of language not as a static, communicable representation of the speaker's intention, but as a system bearing the weight of centuries of intention, motivation, and implication. Language can never be molded into working for the speaker's unique purpose but can only be handed back and forth like printed books borrowed from a lending library. Since language is already composed of weighted uses, grammatical rules, and agreed conventional lexis, Bakhtin regards it as negating the uniqueness of personal experience, and with it any possibility of maintaining a connection with value and intention, as does Sartre in *Being and Nothingness*: "the meaning of my expression always escapes me. I never know if I signify what I wish to signify. . . . As soon as I express myself, I can only guess at the meaning of what I express, i.e. the meaning of what I am" (37).

Within every single word, within every single utterance, Bakhtin identifies a large and ancient concatenation of ideas, motives, and intentions utilized by centuries of speakers and writers. All language, according to Bakhtin, is pre-stratified into social dialects, characteristic group behavior, professional jargons, languages of generations and age-groups, tendentious languages, languages of authority, and, especially in recent media language, the discourse of various circles and passing fashions of the day, even of the hour.[3]

Bakhtin finds himself unable to describe social forms and conventions (what most critics today would define as "genres") without reducing them to the obviously individualistic category of "voices," and equally unable to imagine consistent dialogue among similar genres, or among works within a genre, except as a kind of loose, multiform whole. He reserves the term *genre* for obvious, widely accepted generic structures—epic, myth, poetry, or the space–time structures of youth, age, the beginning, the end, and so on. Essentially, *genre* in Bakhtin is something of a nonce-word. He seems ultimately to suggest that it is possible—indeed, necessary—to reduce *all* forms, narratives, structures, and so on, to their own ideological languages. Nevertheless, he keeps the terms *genre* and *generic wholes* to identify and theorize widely accepted forms, partly in order to enable reference to wider literary and narrative traditions than his consistent return to sociological and ideological theory would generate.

As Ken Hirschkop and David Shepherd point out, even the meanings of words like *dialogism* and *carnival* are a sedimentation of past uses, current and past social conflicts, the changing forms of ideological life; in short, these terms are themselves dialogical (11). Yet this does not, of course, mean that the schema at play in even the most basic language-unit are too densely interwoven ever to be understood. Such is the fleeting language of a day, of an epoch, a social group, a genre, a school and so forth, writes Bakhtin, that "[i]t is possible to give a concrete and detailed analysis of any utterance, once having exposed it as a contradiction-ridden, tension-filled unity of & embattled tendencies in the life of language" (DN 272).

Style Magazines

In today's popular culture, nowhere is the influence of what Bakhtin describes as polyglossia more obvious and immediate than in contemporary style magazines like *Details*, *The Face*, *Stuff*, *Wallpaper* and *i-D*. These magazines provide a blend of interviews (with people involved in film, fashion, and music), articles (on sport, television, and clothes), and breezy chat (about style and shopping). They all have an international readership; in the West, they are sold in outlets like Borders and Barnes & Noble, and in other countries they can be purchased by subscription, and on the Internet.

The polyglossia of these magazines consistently obliterates the distinctions, on the written page, between high-artistic-noncommercial and mass-pop-consumerist, between street and catwalk fashions, art and advertising, poetry and lyrics, comic-strip and literature, the marginal and the mainstream. It is often rather difficult to tell fashion shots from advertisement photographs, and sometimes virtually impossible to distinguish between magazine articles, and commercials designed to mimic the magazine's particular editorial style (see figures 1.1–1.4). The prose is usually a fusion of colloquialisms, technical jargon, street talk, intellectual analysis, abbreviations, and fashionable puns. In this extract from British magazine *The Face*, for example, film critic Jim McClellan reviews a Percy Adlon film, *Rosalie Goes Shopping*:

> A comic fantasy about the consumer credit trap and the personal computer, it stars Marianne Sagebrecht as a German housewife determined to live life the shop-till-you-drop postmodern American way. Hubbie Brad Davis's wages can't even pay the interest on all those afternoons at the mall, so she starts double-dealing with a vast deck of credit cards and number-crunching on her personal computer. Trouble is, her crimes don't seem wrong. *Rosalie* ends up nearly saying something about the hyperconformist consumer and the double standards of the debt economy. Pity about the soundtrack, though.

Figure 1.1 Article on Veronica Webb

Figure 1.2 Article on Matty Hanson

Here, the reviewer's language consists of a fusion of British middle-class colloquialisms ("Hubbie") and ellipsis ("Pity about . . ."), the language of economic reportage ("the consumer credit trap," "the double standards of the debt economy"), "objective journalism"

Figure 1.3   Fasion spread by Brett Dee

("A comic fantasy, it stars Marianne Sagebrecht as a German house-wife"), clichés ("shop-till-you-drop"), the Americanisms commonly used by British journalists ("Trouble is . . . ," "number-crunching") and a parody of current critical sociological and literary discourse ("postmodern American way," "the hyperconformist consumer").[4]

Each stratification of discourse inevitably incorporates various motives, leanings, intentions—unconscious, pre-reflective ideologies that are often defined as political. Bakhtin himself, in a string of dialogues from 1934 onward, moves on to define dialogism as the unmasking of social languages (I. 11). So while this film review, as a contemporary form of polyglossia, constitutes an interweaving of leftist economics, anticapitalism, anticonsumerism, and fashionable British anti-Americanism (although the use of American colloquialisms suggests, on another level, an undercurrent of pro-American sentiment), what these strata perhaps most clearly convey is the discourse of the white, western, middle-class, formally educated male. Ken Hirschkop extends this notion of conflicting ideologies into straight political tendencies: If each language is a voice, then society is a welter of intersecting groups and different ideologies, more or less the version of culture on offer from liberalism, write Hirschkop and Shepherd. And yet things are in a way even worse than that. For each point of view is described as an *interested* point of view: it embodies not just a perspective but a set of values or desires (20).

By referring to an *interested* point of view, however, it seems more likely that Bakhtin is suggesting an unconscious, ideological worldview rather than the active political aims Hirschkop and Shepherd suggest in their use of evaluative terms like *worse*. In "Discourse in the Novel," a similar point is made: "all languages . . . whatever the principle underlying them and making each unique, are specific points of view on the world, forms for conceptualizing the world in words, specific world views, each characterized by its own objects, meanings and values" (DN 291–292).

The main point about polyglossia is that all language has a sideways glance, and yet in Jim McClellan's film review, as in much of the writing in style magazines, the sideways glance seems to be partly directed at itself. This kind of language is self-referential, self-regarding—aware, in a way, of its own shifting polyglossia. The result of this self-parody, which in style magazines such as the self-confessedly superficial *The Face* seems almost inevitable, is that the language loses much of its primary intention (here, the film review) and develops instead into a game of words, a kind of linguistic solitaire. This is the kind of discourse that lives, as it were, beyond itself, "in a living impulse [*napravlenost*] toward the object" (DN 292). Ann Jefferson writes: "Looking (at yourself) while you leap is a highly dangerous thing to do, and on the figurative plain the effects of such self-regarding attitudes can be just as devastating, because they empty acts of their substance and purpose, and *action* is, significantly, turned into *play* or *gesture*" (157).

This kind of ironic, self-reflecting parody of the dialogism inherent in language is often the style of the traditional fool, who mocks others' uses of words by using them himself. Shakespeare's Fool in *King Lear*, for example, is introduced into the text partly for purposes of making strange (*ostranenie*) the world of conventional pathos by forcing Lear's dramatic, aristocratic language of suffering to appear distant and unreal when it is cited beside similar meanings couched in the Fool's own folkloric, nursery riddles.

And this is precisely the relation between dialogism—both lived and textual—and the Bakhtinian notion of carnival. Carnival is the time when all social groups and classes join together in a wild Saturnalian celebration which involves the fusion of each group's dialogical stratum into a parodic, ironic festival of language. According to Bakhtin, each level of polyglossia is linked to the next by a common folkloric laughter, whose roots go back deep into pre-class folklore and which destroys traditional connections and abolishes idealized strata, bringing out the crude, unmediated links between words and concepts that are normally kept very separate. Carnival, according to Bakhtin, represents the disunification of what has traditionally been linked, and the bringing together of that which has been traditionally kept distant and disunified (FT 170).

Carnival, in the written text as well as in lived language, brings the everyday into sacred life in the form of ritualistic violations (*skvernoslovie*), causing ritualistic laughter and clownishness. The slave and jester become substitutes for the ruler and god, various forms of ritualistic parody make their appearance, and the passions are mixed with laughter and gaiety. Bakhtinian carnival cavalierly suppresses hierarchies and distinctions, recalling us to a common creatureliness, as Terry Eagleton puts it ("Bakhtin," 188).

So just as the court jester's ironic repetition of common language estranges that language and alienates it, so at the carnival does the riotous confusion of all varieties of discourse, both high and low, make strange the similar level of dialogism preexistent in language. Opposed to all those who are well-to-do in life, suggests Bakhtin, comes the language of the merry rogue—streetsongs, folksayings, anecdotes, a lively parody of the words of poets, scholars, monks, knights, and others. Like the interplay of genres and levels within the prose of style magazines, the language of the merry rogue parodically reprocesses other people's discourse, but always in such a way as to rob them of their power, to distance them from the mouth, as it were, by means of a roguish deception, to mock their language and thus turn what was direct discourse into light self-parody. "Falsehood is illuminated by ironic consciousness and in the mouth of the happy rogue parodies itself" (DN 402).

In this respect, much of recent popular culture appears as *permanent carnivalization* (though "permanent" in the sense of permanently ephemeral, constantly changing). Style magazines consistently offer a wide range of interweaving discourses, languages, ontologies, and dialogues characteristic of the anti-canonism Bakhtin defines as essential to the language of novelization, and the festival of polyglossia that results is not a mere sideshow at a traveling carnival, but a permanently ephemeral, playful, self-referential, self-parodying component of popular culture. Bakhtin's idea of carnival, both lived and textual, as the self-regarding parody of different language styles and levels of dialogue, and his description of the stock-in-trade carnival jester who has to be able to mimic birds and animals, and the speech, facial expressions and gesticulations of a slave, a peasant, a procurer, a scholastic pedant and a foreigner (PN 57) are highly relevant to pop culture's current and continuous taste for impersonation and parody.

In style magazines, the spirit of carnival manifests itself as parody, pastiche, or irony ("that which cannot be put in words without betraying itself" [I. 33])—a type of folkloric laughter which, Bakhtin believes, works to bring "official," "sacred" things (politics, religion, business)[5] to a place of maximal proximity where they can be turned inside out and closely examined from all angles. In most contemporary style magazines, in fact, all representatives of the established canonical literary system and the old, official, sacred world—judges, lawyers, politicians, churchmen, well-established media figures—are treated as absurd and ridiculous and laughed down in favor of the latest top model, movie star, or cult musician, kings and queens for an issue precisely because of their hip, chic, ephemeral nature. By way of example, consider how style magazines feature the latest independent bands like Whitewash or The Monkfish, spotlighted usually because their refusal to sign up to any major record label virtually guarantees their status as flash-in-the-pan, up-to-the-minute underground fads, never likely to become main-stream acts.

At other times, this carnivalesque impulse takes the form of a mock-ery of "intellectual" prose and criticism. In such cases, the language of the writer strives to overcome literariness and to get away from outmoded styles and period-bound language by fusing this very literariness with street talk, creating a dialogue between the canonical literary system and the generic languages of various subcultures, making language parody itself.

Indeed, the key to much pop culture today lies in the aesthetic (or, often, anti-aesthetic) avowal of superficiality, of vacancy, of *as little meaning as possible*. Style magazines like *The Face*, its very title heralding an uncompromising superficiality, are temples to ephemera, to the garish colors and images of a transient, drifting pop life. These magazines, like pop videos and television ads, are not meant to be read or studied closely, but to be "cruised" through, looked at fleetingly with a vague sense of admiration and temptation, the same way you might gaze at a shop window display of seductive, brightly colored consumer goods until, like Rosalie in *Rosalie Goes Shopping*, you become a "hyperconformist consumer in the shop-till-you-drop postmodern American way."

Here, it is important to distinguish between carnival as a vast mélange of styles, which lends itself well enough to postmodernism, and carnival as political animus. In other words, to graft Bakhtinian carnival onto postmodern culture without reservation brings the latter out as rather more subversive than much of it actually is. Rather than providing an active force of radicalism, the carnivalesque destroys epic distance and restores a dynamic authenticity (EN 35) to man, allowing participants to investigate themselves freely, to study the disparity between their potential and their reality, in the text as well as on the street. Bakhtin talks about the performances of obscenely cavorting phallophors in religious processions, and *deikilists* (mimers) who both travestied national and local myths, and mimicked the characteristically typical languages and speech mannerisms of foreign doctors, procurers, heterae, peasants, slaves, scholars, judges, and so on (see PN 41–83).

The Chronotope of Youth

An article on the resurgent popularity of the T-shirt in *Details* is accompanied by artistic photos of vague-looking models. A few pages later, a nine-page photographic fashion supplement features similar images of slightly puzzled, slightly aloof-looking, "artistic" characters. The models used are always young and bone-thin, the writers affect a youthful idiom, the pop music featured is always new, and played by young musicians. The films and books reviewed are the latest hip releases, the outlandish clothes modeled could be worn only by the very young. The ads (for new bank accounts, cosmetics, sound systems and stereos, diet products) and notices (of upcoming concerts, shows, new clubs, independent movies) are all aimed at an audience under thirty. Style magazines seem permanently suspended in their own dream of youth-time, where the interests and concerns of older and less chic generations (marriage, the family, jobs, health, children, finances, the home) are featured only parodically, as subjects for comedy, and are otherwise dismissed as of interest only to the readers of other, more adult magazines like *GQ* or *Vogue*.

This permanent existence in a vacuum of youth-time resembles a kind of generic whole which Bakhtin in his studies on the novel refers to as the *chronotope* (space-time: according to Bakhtin every entry into the sphere of meaning is accomplished only through the gates of the chronotope). In the novel, the chronotope can take a variety of forms: Bakhtin mentions chronotopes of the road, the threshold, the castle, the family idyll. Style magazines like *Details* and *i-D* present an eternal chronotope of youth, of youth adventure, the folkloric conception of the idealized *beginning*, youth idyll with its magic costumes and accoutrements, cosmetics, fashionable clothes, pop music, certain brands of drink. The youth idyll presented in style magazines is a characteristic of folkloric time charted against the background of the reader's own, contemporary perception of time.

Bakhtin points out in "Forms of Time and Chronotope in the Novel" that our understanding of folkloric time is not a fact of primitive man's consciousness, but rather something that must be adduced from a study of objective material, since the chronotope is what determines the unity of every motif and idea in a text, as well as determining the logic by which these images unfold. The chronotope, then, is artifical—the youth idyll of the style magazine, for example, exhibits no teenage acne, no young people who are not thin and beautiful, no older artists or musicians, no youthful suicide, depression, or psychological breakdown except when angst and neurosis are chic.

This filtering of moments in chronotope, Hirschkop and Shepherd believe, takes place not because all authors are necessarily prejudiced, but because they must approach the object language with some task, project, or aim in mind if speech is to exhibit ideological structure (23). The reasoning behind each motif of youth chronotope selected for a magazine article, pop song, or advertisement, then, is connected to the capitalist nature of the market in which these texts are sold and the fact that they are almost universally produced as commercial commodities. Consequently, it would be unwise to empty Bakhtin's carnival theory of its political conflict, to reduce it to an eclectic blend of styles and languages, to see it as conflation rather than contention, as generalized indifference rather than the clash of highly interested standpoints.

Punk and Carnival

There is a great deal of carnival spirit in the more aggressive forms of popular culture, notably in the punk, goth, and grunge movements often celebrated in style magazines, where ritualistic violation and cultic indecency are all part of the act. Like the carnival jester, goth, grunge, and punk rockers are Lords of Misrule who celebrate a thoughtless deceit opposed to everything they find to be conventional and false—synthetic forms for the parodied exposure of others. As the harbinger of carnival, the punk, like the clown, is granted "the right *not* to understand, the right to confuse, the right to parody others while talking, the right not to be taken literally, the right to act life as a comedy and to treat others as actors, the right to rip off masks, the right to rage at others with a primeval (almost cultic) rage" (FT 163).

One important function of this spirited, self-conscious dialogism is to reduce all false sublimations back to their earthy, earthly roots. As in Menippean satire, the cruder, more bawdy, brawling, more obviously mocking forms of carnival bring everything down to a single level, like those rap singers whose lyrics consist of the ritualisted repetition of profanities. Bakhtin points out that laughter is associated with folklore and the gross realities of life, possessing the capacity to strip the object of the false verbal and ideological husk that encloses it (see FT 158–224)—a carnival performance which realizes the theories of both the textual and linguistic carnivalesque.

The Sex Pistols (see figure 1.4), the original punk rockers, sang, of course, about bodies, and one of their slogans was "Fuck Forever." In fact, most of the punk movement's original motivation centered around an impulse to disgust and appall by reducing the sublimations of serious artists and musicians to a celebration of what Bakhtin describes as "the series of the human body" (FT 170). Typical punk acts included vomiting (the food series), wearing trash bags held together with safety-pins (the human clothing series), getting "pissed" to "destroy" (the drink and drunkenness series), fucking forever (the sexual series), and—after the death of the Sex Pistols bassist, Sid Vicious, in 1979—sporting "Sid Lives" T-shirts (the death series). "The pleasures of carnival," write Hirschkop and Shepherd, "are not the pleasures of mere talk but those of a discourse that has rediscovered its connection to the concrete" (35). Here, again, we see the fusion of textual carnivalesque with the carnivalesque in performance to form the polyglossia of texts and forms of language more usually excluded from the literary system.

Much of this ideological mode of carnivalization, of course, revolves around the destruction of images sacred in other, different, often opposing

Figure 1.4   The Sex Pistols, from *The Great Rock and Roll Swindle* (Julien Temple, 1980)

cultural levels and dialogues. Just as advertisements in style magazines, through a process of ritual disembowelment, use celebrated and highly revered images (old masters, pieces of "high art") for what is often considered to be the rather trivial process of selling, things held sacred in one language or discourse are inevitably parodied in another. For example, the Sex Pistols made use of material that is sacrilegious to other dialogues. Their lyrics made fun out of the monarchy ("God Save the Queen"), the government ("Anarchy in the U.K."), the human body ("Bodies"), multinational corporations ("EMI"), and the holocaust ("Belsen was a Gas"). Manager Malcolm McLaren's sale of "Sid Lives" T-shirts only a couple of weeks after the bassist's heroin overdose smacks a great deal of Bakhtin's carnivalesque version of death, which he applies particularly to Rabelaisian burlesque ("in the grotesque [clownish] portrayal of death, the image of death itself takes on humorous aspects: *death* is inseparable from *laughter*" [FT 196]).

That once-taboo topics like sex and death can be treated with such hilarity during the carnival is a signifier not just of the carnivalesque reduction of all cultural sublimations to their folkloric roots, but, even further, the desecration of all that a culture considers sacred or meaningful to no more than another of the merry rogue's clownish jests. Everything that has been built up to have significance and moment for mankind is rendered absurd: there is an emphasis in the carnivalesque on the healthy failure of the fool (the man of the people) to understand accepted conventions and falsehoods (religion, the government, education, capitalism, advertising), which expose them for what they really are. Here, again, there is little difference between textual and lived carnivalesque. Textual polyglossia— the fusion of canonical and non-canonical literary and subliterary systems—is embodied in the performance of real life. The punk, for example, estranges the discourse of mass-appeal, major-label, commercialized chart music by means of an uncomprehending stupidity (simplicity, naïvété), where the very aspect of not understanding, not *grasping* the conventions of a society, not *comprehending* lofty, meaning-charged lyrics, chords, words, labels, and events, remains vital.

Forms of the carnivalesque and examples of polyglot novelization in text are generally characterized by a self-evident failure to "stand up" to philosophical literary theories, but are simultaneously of value for their capacity for "breaking down" into infinite layers of dialogical strata to reveal the limits and constraints of such definitions which restrict, for example, a variety of polyglot texts from inclusion in a traditionally narrow literary canon. Like the anti-academic, anti-serious, anti-intelligent Saturnalian humor of the punk movement and its music, much of contemporary popular culture is joyously aware of the inadequacies of its own language. For example, in its gleeful celebration of pop art, pop journalism, pop cinema, pop advertising, pop literature, pop feminism, and pop shopping, the discourse of magazines like *Details*, *The Face*, and *i-D*, is a joke at the expense of its own irrelevance, its own unimportance, its own meaninglessness, its own ephemeral chic.

Such polyglot texts recognize the emptiness of society, the plasticity of consumerism and, like the Sex Pistols singing about their own vacancy ("Pretty Vacant") or their manager Malcolm McLaren making a film entitled *The Great Rock and Roll Swindle* (and, not coincidentally, profiting financially from his rebellion), resolve that there is nothing left to do but to celebrate that very vacancy, to go shopping. In fact, in playful acknowledgment of their sell-out, the Sex Pistols reunion tour in 1996 was labelled "The Filthy Lucre Tour," and shares in the venture were floated on the British stock exchange.

Comic-Ironic Counterparts

For Bakhtin, this ambivalent image of wise ignorance brings to mind the self-praise of the Socratic dialogue ("I am wiser than everyone, because I know that I know nothing"), and the image of Socrates ("a wise man of the most elevated sort," "wearing the popular mask of a bewildered fool [almost a *Margit*]" [EN 24]). There is no sort of direct discourse, suggests Bakhtin—artistic, rhetorical, philosophical, everyday[6]—that doesn't have its own parodying and travestying double, its own comic–ironic *contre-partie*" (PN 53).

In this light, pop culture appears as the reverse of "high" culture, its alter ego, wherein all pretensions to meaning, relevance, and aesthetic value are travestied by a parodic, mocking dialogue of vacancy, anti-aestheticism and the realm of the synthetic. Bakhtin observes that the most wise and revered figures in epic have their comic counterparts, and become themselves comic: "Odysseus . . . donned a clown's fool's cap (*pileus*) and harnessed his horse and conquered death in battle . . . descended into the nether world [to become] the monstrous glutton, the playboy, the drunk and scrapper, but especially Hercules the madman" (PN 54).

The discourse of style magazines—where pop art, music, fashion, and literature all parody their more serious counterparts and where monarchs and political leaders are mocked by figures like Eminem and Marilyn Manson, the Lords of Misrule, becomes what Bakhtin describes as the Holiday of Fools or *festa stultorum*, a form of *ludus* in which everything is reversed, even clothing; trousers were worn on the head, for instance, an operation that symbolically reflects in some measure the jongleurs, who are depicted in miniatures head-downward (PN 72): a dialogue between what the given system will admit into its canons, and what it systematically rejects—forms of language embraced by Bakhtin as polyglossia. Everything serious has to have a comic double, in text and in reality. Just as in the Saturnalia the clown is the double of the master, similar comic doubles exist in all forms of literature and culture. And just as the Lord of Misrule doubles as the king, the funhouse of the style magazine represents the parodic, self-referential, carnivalesque counterpart to all forms of high culture.

Carnival and Madness

And yet perhaps neither phenomenon, carnival nor popular culture, is as unqualifiedly positive as it seems to be, since this systemic reversal or inversion figured by the carnivalesque can also be interpreted as a kind of madness. There is a constant similarity between the polyglossia of the carnival, textual and nontextual, and the manifold layers and levels of discourse within the lunatic's psychological dialogism. Clair Wills, in her feminist interpretation of carnival, draws a parallel between the carnival itself, which disrupts by juxtaposing public indecency with official order, and women's texts considered hysteric even by avant-garde writers such as Julia Kristeva.

Wills charts a connection between carnival, which fuses common and official types of discourse as well as many others in a polyglossia, and the hysteric's reliving of past history, family situations, and so on, in the present: her capacity for turning things upside-down is contained within the family. The transgressive nature of popular festive forms and hysterical discourse are connected not only in their similar relation to history, but in their content: "Freud's descriptions of the hysteric call on popular festive imagery: it is striking how the broken fragments of carnival, terrifying and disconnected, glide through the discourse of the hysteric" (133).

This kind of hysteria—a form of polyglossia in its anti-canonical dialogue between what the given system admits as the language of literature and what it rejects as subculture—manifests itself not only in the fusion of retrospective and up-to-the-minute language in style magazines but, more clearly perhaps, in the continuous, repetitive, confused stream of discourse that comes from the radio D. J., nightclub M. C., or rap artists like Eminem and 50 Cent. Wills views the discourse of the hysteric as an attempt to open up the protests of the women of the past by seeing their similarity with the feminist protest of the present (149), just as Bakhtinian carnival brings together the language of the past and the present. "The crises of the past," writes Wills, "live on in a separate area of the psyche like the last vestiges of a small-town market-place carnival" (136). In *The Newly Born Woman*, Hélène Cixous and Catherine Clément cite Marcel Mauss to describe people with a dangerous symbiotic mobility as afflicted with what she calls "madness, anomaly, perversion," people whom Mauss labels "neurotics, ecstatics, outsiders, carnies, drifters, jugglers, acrobats" (7).

This interpretation of carnival as insanity, where the fusing strands of each type of polyglottal discourse represent the lunatic's reliving of past events, emotions, lives, and dialogues, bodes ill for popular culture. If the polyglossia of today's pop culture is symptomatic of a carnivalesque madness, then that madness is accepted—indeed, worshiped—all over the Western world. If the interplay between official, unofficial, popular, parodic, journalistic, artistic, vulgar, colloquial, and other forms of textual and nontextual discourse is to be interpreted as symptomatic of the hysteric's revertive, transgressive reliving of past and other dialogues, then the hysteria of popular culture is a fundamental part of everyday life in the Western world.

And this is where any application of Bakhtinian analysis of the carnivalesque to textual practices encounters a stumbling block. So far in this chapter, I have been referring to carnivalesque practices in text and reality as realizing similar effects. However, the textual carnival can never completely realize the dialogical struggle current in the social carnival. Although their effects and implications may be similar, it will never be possible to align completely the carnivalesque in text and the carnivalesque in performance, unless the solitary activity of reading is regarded as a very special kind of performance.

However joyous and festive they may appear, commodities of the textual carnivalesque—those artifacts that emphasize words and language rather than being and doing—are still no more than static products, inevitably far distanced from the active, participatory reality they attempt to imitate on the page. There is a vast difference between the text which promotes the carnivalesque in linguistic terms, and the actual carnival itself. Clair Wills is hasty to criticize the lack of connections between the textual carnival and the carnivalesque as a genuine social force. Similarly, Ann Jefferson agrees that authoring is by its very nature a decarnivalizing activity, since the authorial perspective and the demarcation between the observer and participants are against the whole spirit of carnival.

Bakhtin's interpretation of what he refers to as the novel, defined by a proclivity to display different languages interpenetrating one another, allows examples of language outside the bounds of what traditional scholars would think of as strictly *literary* history, such as the discourse of style magazines, to be studied as important instances of polyglossia. Nevertheless, no text can come closer to carnival than the levels of description, imitation, and representation. There is always some kind of dichotomy between the carnivalesque discourses of the text and the social power of its actual equivalent—the rock festival, the grunge concert, the mosh pit, the all-night party: the realities of being and doing.

However, it is important to remember Bakhtin's words: "great novelistic images continue to grow and develop even after the moment of their creation; they are capable of being creatively transformed in different eras, far distant from the day and hour of their original birth" (DN 422). Rather than simply subscribing to the cliché of "different times, different interpretations," Bakhtin is suggesting that the polyglossia of all language structures in all dialogic texts, irrespective of origin and original purpose, allows them to be given new relevance, new meaning, new interest, as they are subjected, like the texts used in this study, to new readings and new analysis.

It is this independent, interdependent battle and play of different levels and layers of interested dialogue that gives every text a variety of meanings, interpretations, subtexts. This quality of inherent polyglossia means that texts produced for very direct and immediate purposes like hyped-up, overexposed commercialism of style magazines, in other times and contexts, come to assume a radically different meaning. But their meaning is still a textual meaning, their dialogism a textual dialogism. In the place of the powerful, social polyglossia of the *real* carnival, all we can observe instead is what Ann Jefferson describes as "the lonely carnival of reading" (174).

CHAPTER 2

JOYFUL MAYHEM: BAKHTIN AND FOOTBALL FANS

The clamor and chanting of a large crowd of football fans embodies, to many people, all that they most fear and loathe: drunken, bawdy, brawling male youths violating public peace and privacy by howling out their trivial allegiances. It is my suspicion that any anathematized subculture must be extremely powerful in the way it so easily threatens all levels and elements of society. In this chapter, I hope to discover some of the reasons how and in what ways the subculture of football fans functions to demolish piety, and thereby to disrupt the official solemnity of the status quo. Any phenomenon so threatening must, it seems, be also somehow meaningful in its presentation of radical and often unpopular views addressing social, political, racial, and sexual inequities, thereby airing explicit versions of normally repressed ideas about society, its valuations, and ideologies.

If the games of the folk devil are not simply random manifestations of thoughtless impulses to violence and disruption, then neither are they too shifting, trivial, or transient to have any lasting effect. In this chapter, I want to understand precisely what it is about the distancing and degrading nature of the football fan that has allowed this particular branch of urban subculture to become so forcefully stigmatized. I approach this question by looking at some of the ways in which the subculture of football fans relates to parent societies and other traditions. I also consider the dynamic and contradictory associations between football and commercial phenomena, including media images and stereotypes, and examine the affiliations between the culture of football, and tangential political and ideological issues. The aim of this chapter is to discover whether the displaced, marginalized, and autonomized subculture of the football fan is not, in fact, a regulated and hierarchical form of festivity ordered by a set of rules governing its aesthetic practice, whose anarchic and carnivalesque impulse is carefully channeled by a series of regularities and graduated levels.

Football and Carnival

The public, ritualistic, performative subculture of the football fan—its relation to the present and to reality, its primitivistic celebration of simplicity and timelessness, and its integrity of form—require access to some highly ambiguous social functions, both subversive and conservative. Bakhtin's readings of the carnivalesque allow for a more thoughtful and sensitive understanding of the ambivalent behavior of football fans than that provided by the discourse of social studies or ideology. Bakhtin's approach would seem to suggest that the subcultural performance comes alive and communicates only when the participants provide it with their own interpretations and understandings, a conclusion similar to that reached by scholars working on television and popular media audiences, such as Janice Radway (1991) and Tania Modelski (1986), both of whom work with feminist reception theory.

The argument that the behavior of football fans can best be understood as an example of the Bakhtinian carnivalesque necessarily excludes other rhetorical methods. It also excludes other methods of cultural performance study, such as social drama analysis, that might seem appropriate inroads of access to this fascinating area of popular culture. It seems to me, however, that Bakhtin's method is the most effective—not only because it pays special attention to the foregrounding of laughter, humor, irony, and elements of self-parody, but also because there are some very obvious connections between Bakhtinian carnival, as described in "Discourse in the Novel," and the nature of competitive football.

There is a striking resemblance, for example, in terms of special, *sacred* time in the flow of secular (*working*) time, and a suspension of the convention of secular time, usually at some time on a Saturday afternoon. The football stadium itself is also a kind of *sacred space* within secular space—and, moreover, like many other forms of subcultures, football fandom is *regulated* festivity. The anarchic, carnivalesque charge is confined within a carefully policed stadium, just as in medieval carnival there were set limits to the time allowed for such activities, with ritualistic reintroductions back into "normal" ecclesiastical and official time and space.

In her work on Bakhtin, Linda Hutcheon (1988) has pointed out that there is something quite ironic about the fact that the carnivalesque involves rigid regularities, discrete groups, graduated hierarchies and so on, which brings up the question of just how *carnivalesque* this kind of structured, rigorous, hierarchical festivity really is (what Deleuze has called the *haecceity* [*thisness*] of the particular configuration of circumstances at each particular event may well be helpful here). It could possibly be argued that football fandom is really only a parodic protest, which links up, following Hutcheon, with the idea of carnival as a *safety valve*, with an essentially *conservative* function socially. It would be unwise to forget that the potential of carnival for radical rebellion is in the end politically limited, since it is, after all, *licensed* misrule, a contained and officially sanctioned rebellion, after which everybody goes back to work.

There are further arresting analogies between football and Bakhtinian carnival. In "Discourse in the Novel," Bakhtin discovers that carnival is broadly popular in its potential inclusiveness (occurring as it does within an "unraised" place, a "public square," not unlike the football stadium). Analogously, the rituals of the football fan fit readily into theories of carnival because they consist broadly of practices culled from the "lower spheres" of life (what Bakhtin refers to as "Socratic degradations")—the fields of tradesmen and everyday actions, which serve to bring the world closer in order for us to examine it fearlessly. Tailgate parties, face-painting, the decorating of vehicles in team colors, mock fights, chants and dances, the brandishing of banners and mascots—these are all public, communal activities. The aim of the carnivalesque, according to Bakhtin in *Problems of Dostoyevsky's Poetics*, is "to feed on dense experience: to be with the smell of real human bodies" (47).

Fight Songs and Jock Jams

One of the most common behavioral patterns of football fans involves the singing of either older, traditional fight songs, or contemporary jock jams, often accompanied by shouts of encouragement and disappointment, warlike chanting, and yells of victory or defeat. A rhetorical method of analysis would focus on the role of language, tropes, semantics, and so on within the performance of such songs, but in the case of modern football, such an analysis seems redundant. Whereas these songs *do* contain linguistic idiosyncrasies and so forth (in the narrow sense), they are generally of secondary importance and in this genre acquire special functions that are oblique. Bakhtin, on the other hand, pays special attention to how language provides a kind of identity and a belief in a sense of collective community. He observes how such forms of polyglossia involve an indeterminacy, a semantic open-endedness, a living contact with unfinished, still-evolving contemporary reality and the ongoing present.

Of course, all forms of subcultures are not necessarily *by definition* dialogical, just as all "high" culture is not necessarily monological, and there are a variety of distinctions to be made between different types of subcultures and the different layers and levels of dialogism they involve. Once a form of dialogism has been identified, however, it never remains merely as one form as "construction of the whole" (Bakhtin's interpretative definition of *genre*) among others, nor does it co-relate with other genres in peaceful or harmonious coexistence. Instead, it aids the novelization of other genres and helps to bring them into the zone of novelization.

Fight songs and jock jams can be heard in all countries where football is a fundamental part of the national culture. Songs and chants in support of a team are developed not to be read or analyzed (or even, for that matter, written down), but to be chanted and sung as part of a ritualistic public performance. They arise from the tradition of folk songs, popular lays, burlesque rhymes, and ballads, and they are related to local, patriotic or nationalistic songs celebrating the supremacy of the singer's hometown, state, or country. The use of ritual argot and slang is linked to the familiar strata of folk language, which plays an enormous part in the formulation of dialogism.

Many scholars have focused their attention on why football fans are predominantly male.[1] In their studies of the environmental psychology of football grounds, for example, sociologists have suggested that the male obsession with football relates directly to the boredom of so much of male working-class social life, and to its Puritanism. Also, it has been suggested that social hierarchies contribute to providing the carnival urge, particularly the elitist structure of the football stadium, where seats can be significantly different in terms of price, comfort, and view.

Other scholars have pointed out that the irreverence of the singing fan provides a direct challenge to institutionalized forms of politeness. They argue that the spontaneity and lack of formality of these songs and jams highlights the restrictions of a bureaucratic, neighbor-watching conformism away from the stadium. It would then follow that the piratical, outrageous air of the excited fan finds its meaning and clumsy grace from what Bakhtin refers to as the "ludicrous orderedness" of the rest of us. Another explanation for the phenomenon comes perhaps paradoxically from the sports fan's sensed loss in personal autonomy: he is part of a mass, rowdy crowd excluded from "social normality," but at the same time his style mocks and parodies conventional values and implies some kind of superior vision.

Today, most football fans prefer watching the televised coverage of the day's game rather than traveling long distances to sit in a crowded stadium. Although fans at home often create their own domestic rituals around "game day" (such as, inviting friends over, barbecuing, drinking beer, watching the pregame show, and so on), there is still a difference between this kind of behavior and that of the fans who travel to see their teams play at the stadium. The two experiences are only remotely related, but it might be unwise to suggest that football supporting is, any more, a pure folk phenomenon. Like many other popular subcultures, such as pirate radio, independent-label rock music, and fanzines, football supporting, even at the college level, has been colonized by the media, and this must surely alter the ways such forms are now being used (to promote advertising, to increase viewing figures, to encourage factionalism and so on), no matter to what extent they might derive from older folk forms.

Performative Poetics

Bakhtin's analysis of the carnivalesque attends to a number of details that cultural performance studies and social science analysis of subcultures cannot. Part of the appropriateness of this method, as the work done on Bakhtin by other scholars demonstrates, is Bakhtin's recognition of the word as *performed*, which is clearly vital to the understanding of football fans, their symbols, mascots, colors, rituals, and songs. In *Problems of Dostoyevsky's Poetics*, Bakhtin explains his ideas of the carnivalesque in language as a *live event*, played out at the point of a dialogic meeting between two or several consciousnesses, united to the world it describes. Carnivalesque discourse, unlike traditional language, does not mirror the world *mimetically*, but is rather *part* of it, interacts with it to transform discourse, speaker, and audience: "The work and the world represented in it enter the real world and enrich it, and the real world enters the work and its world as part of the process of its creation, as well as part of its subsequent life . . ." (47).

In the same way, fight songs and jock jams are themselves a kind of performance. Even a seemingly accidental, insignificant pretext can serve as an immediate or external starting point for a dialogue or a song. Accidental encounters on the field, news of the latest scores and so on can all serve as impetus for new chants. Many old songs are spontaneously adapted to fit immediate circumstances, often in a comic vein. These range from the most obvious repetitions of new scores, to more complex references. Fans will often develop humorous jokes, songs, and poems either to throw opposing players off their game, or to encourage the home team. Before the game, T-shirts are often printed and distributed that contain obscene slogans ridiculing particular players on the opposing team, or that vilify the team in general. Many fans trying to rattle opposing players are content with boos and the occasional wisecrack; others cross the line between civility and crudeness. This is especially the case when it comes to "superstar" players like Peyton Manning, Randy Moss, and Marshall Faulk, who are regularly singled out for abuse from supporters of the opposing team.

In "Discourse in the Novel," Bakhtin writes about the simplicity and timelessness of traditional ballads, folk songs, and ritual mantras and the ways in which they aid the establishment of self-identity. This is another way in which the carnivalesque lyrics of the fight song are themselves part of a community performance. The anthem of the Philadelphia Eagles, for example, has simple words that are sung throughout the game to a catchy tune played by the pep band:

> Fly Eagles fly, on the road to victory,
> Fight Eagles fight, score a touchdown 1,2,3.
> Hit 'em low, hit 'em high, and watch our Eagles fly.
> Fly Eagles fly, on the road to victory,
> E-A-G-L-E-S—Eagles!

Chants, jingles, and ditties like this one are presumably supposed to bring the rewards of participation, a sense of "being together" in support of a team and sharing a united front against "the others." Whatever the aim of the Phildelphia Eagles' management in promoting this chant at football games—possibly to discourage the singing of other, less welcoming songs—it certainly encourages a participatory performance. Participation in such a voluntary organization as a football fan club is an extremely favorable condition for self-commitment, the enhancing of self-esteem, and the provision of personal satisfaction. Perhaps the Philadelphia Eagles' management, with their small pep band playing a jazzed up version of the ditty over the stadium's sound system, is attempting to replace fighting with chanting as a "natural performance arena" for the exercise of masculine qualities, for the creation of group bonds, and for the development of localized forms of social organization—features that are often posited as the key to football's contemporary importance.

The anthem of the Philadelphia Eagles, as a form of ritual performance mantra, establishes a kind of *united* self-identity ("Watch *our*

Eagles fly"). This song supplies possibilities for the exploitation of a regressive, primitivistic celebration of simplicity and timelessness ("Hit 'em low, hit 'em high"). The history of such subcultural performance utterances can be traced back through the complex roots of ballads and folk songs to a point before tonal conventions had become determining, where repeated conventional cadences provided a rhythmic foundation. The rhythmic regularity of the song's trimeter is an alternative to (say) the iambic pentameter, which stresses the curve of a uniquely individual voice speaking *across* the metrical pattern. Alternatively, the rhythm of the Philadelphia Eagles's fight song points to performance creativity, as opposed to the individualistic voice.

The power of the word to effect its curse or blessing on the subject has always been regarded as an act full of magic significance. Historical remains have shown that curse words etched into wood, dropped into wells, or chalked onto the walls or caves long predate the advent of general literacy. And so in speech and performance: the magical idea that what one says can physically effect the person one says it to survives today in the law of libel and in the nervous shiftings of real and assumed names amongst celebrities and others, and it has always had its counterpart in the idea of the evil eye. Similarly, the singing of jock jams and fight songs signifies entry into the world of ritual and the formal genesis of a respected self. Many of these songs seem to work as ritual mantras of praise and worship, generally of the home team and its supporters, often achieved through the ritualistic degradation of the opposition.

This internal system of ritual order allows fight songs to be adaptable, and popular, pre-accepted songs are used in the creation of new and more immediately relevant ones. Most fight songs are sung to traditional tunes, such as "Camptown Races," or "The Battle Hymn of the Republic." Like their lyrics, the tunes to fight songs tend to be interchangeable. These traditional, popular, and widely known tunes are well-established in the way they influence feeling and emotion by "taking over" and performing disorganized excitement, emotions, and an electric atmosphere in a way that is perhaps impossible in noncarnivalized, nonperformance speech. A similar effect is presumably obtained through similar communal activities, such as fans driving their cars in a long procession into the stadium, beer drinking, tailgate parties, flag and banner waving, and the use of team mascots.

Until fairly recently, football teams that had Native American names, such as Redskins, Braves, Chiefs, Redmen, Savages, and so on, featured as their mascots warlike "Indian Chiefs" who performed make-believe

"Indian dances" dressed in buckskin and full eagle-feather regalia. Fans of these teams would whoop it up, wearing headdresses and war paint, and often brandishing tomahawks. On college campuses with Indian-named teams, fraternity and sorority members would perform "buck and squaw" dances at tailgate parties. While the fans claimed they were "dignifying and honoring" the Indian, Native American groups felt otherwise; most of the teams once known as Chiefs, Braves, Redskins, and Warriors have now selected less controversial names and mascots.

Comedy and Creativity

An area to which many performance scholars of Bakhtin have been perhaps inevitably drawn is his characterization of the relationship between performance and laughter. In "Discourse in the Novel," Bakhtin argues that "the common people's creative culture of laughter" is "the broadest and richest of rituals" (52). In *Rabelais and His World*, he asserts that this kind of parodic-travestying form of laughter sets us free:

> It is, after all, a festive laughter. Therefore it is not an individual reaction to some isolated "comic" event. Carnival laughter is the laughter of all people. Second, it is universal in scope; it is directed at all and everyone, including the carnival's participants; the entire world is seen in its droll aspect, in its gay relativity. Third, this laughter is ambivalent: it is gay, triumphant, and at the same time mocking, deriding. It asserts and denies, it buries and revives. Such is the laughter of the carnival. (11–12)

A social or environmental psychology approach to the role of this kind of carnivalesque laughter within subcultures cannot fully analyze its *performative* function. On the other hand, a cultural performance approach may well fail to understand that this kind of laughter is, above all, a *libidinal* reflex. By drawing our attention to this aspect of laughter in various texts and cultures, Bakhtin shows us how it has a deep philosophical meaning and represents one of the essential forms of truth concerning history and humanity. Thus, because it is an interior form of truth, laughter has implications for the *form* that culture *assumes*. In *Rabelais and his World*, Bakhtin suggests that the various kinds of folkloric laughter liberate the consciousness from the confines of its own discourse, and thereby create freedom.

Through their fight songs, chants, ditties, and jock jams, many football fans put on a burlesque show, a performative parody of generic styles. These parodic and travestying forms keep alive the memory of an ancient struggle, and are continually animated by an ongoing process of stratification and diversification. A large percentage of fight songs and jock jams, for example, are comic or parodic and paradoxical. To fill in traveling time on the buses carrying fans to "away" games, group leaders with bullhorns are usually actively engaged in trying out new versions of old songs and jams, or in making new ones up from scratch. Those songs that meet with approval are tried out at the game, and, if found to have some power, eventually make their way to the stadium where they will be yelled through the bullhorns at the opposition.

The main function of carnivalesque laughter within subcultures seems to be to *uncrown* or *contemporize*. Uncrowning is aimed at direct representation (or, in Bakhtin's words, "living reality"), and involves travesties of all lofty models embodied in NFL myths. Star players, the coach, the team's manager, and even the team itself are *contemporized* and *brought low* by the fan, represented on a plane equal with that of contemporary life, in an everyday environment, in the "low" language of contemporaneity where "common men" like football heroes (Joe Montana) and anti-heroes (O. J. Simpson) can be worshiped or reviled *en masse*. Consequently, carnivalized legends spring up around the heroization (or anti-heroization) of the *common man* who becomes both hero and jester. Individuals like John Elway and Brett Favre become gods, the mythologized subjects of NFL folklore.

According to Bakhtin, carnivalesque laughter occurs in the zone of maximum familiar and crude contact. Laughter during the football game, as in other subcultures, generally leads to what Bakhtin would describe as a "necessary uncrowning," a removal of the object (such as the opposition team, or its star players) from a distanced plane, and an assault on or destruction of the distanced plane in general. Walter Benjamin in *Illuminations* contrasts this up-closeness with the distancing "aura" of the traditional work of art, suggesting how laughter draws an object up close to be examined, demolishing fear and piety before the world, so that it becomes an object of familiar contact (and there are a number of interesting similarities between Bakhtin's and Benjamin's thinking in this area).

In the football stadium, this kind of laughter, comedy, and serio-comedy develops and arises from the inconsistencies and tensions between rival fan groups. It is full of paradoxes, parodies, and travesties, is multi-styled, and often involves elements of polyglossia. In other words, laughter opens things up for free investigation. On the plane of the carnivalesque, it is possible to disrespectfully "walk round" whole objects, and therefore the back and rear portions of an object assume a special importance; consider the popular practice of "mooning" (displaying the buttocks) from supporters' buses at football games. There is an important relation between this kind of humor and modernist techniques—collage, cubism, and montage.

The function of uncrowning is particularly notable when the humor is of a crude or offensive variety, as in the comic fight songs which parody public incidents, such as scandals involving team players, like Michael Irvin's arrest for possession of cocaine, or the trials of Rae Carruth and Ray Lewis. The tone of these chants and ditties involves a parodic and deliberate kind of bad taste that enables the fans to deal with disturbing events. As in punk and other areas of carnival, the mocking of death is a prominent theme (described at length in Bakhtin's *Rabelais and his World*), possible relating to fantasies of immortality. In both the lyrics and performances of such songs, it is often difficult to decide whether "sacred" words—such as references to the chosen team, the team coach and the game itself—are being used *favorably*, or whether there is a familiar, parodic "game of words" in progress. Put in another way, it is difficult to tell if names are being evoked in reverence or in sacrilege. It is, moreover, difficult to determine the degree of license evoked in this "play," which will vary from performance to performance. The sacred becomes sacreligious at different times depending on who is doing the singing, and the impact of the performance may change completely when it is enacted by fans of different teams.

Ritualized Acts of Violence

Uncrowning generally leads to abuse, and abuse can often lead to blows. The question whether or not these violent chants encourage violence at football games has attracted a good deal of attention and academic research. These studies seem to suggest that the connection between sports and violent crime is generally a matter of context. What counts as violent, hooligan-style behavior for some is merely high spirits for others. Indeed, some forms of apparently aggressive fan behavior, widely regarded as manifestations of hooliganism and violence, appear to be a more or less spontaneous expressions of elation, dejection, frustration, anger, and so on, generated by the ups and downs of the game. The truth is that media mythologies of football violence are not borne out by statistical evidence.

Bakhtin's reading of the innate connections between word and *performance* enable us to confront this issue directly. Whether violent words are accompanied by violent actions or not, Bakhtin, aware that language is not merely the mirror of society but the major force in constructing what we perceive and perform in reality, would argue that the violent performance is embedded in the word itself. In short, performative violence is innately embedded in violent words. In *Rabelais and his World*, Bakhtin explains that the exaggerated violence of folk songs is ". . . a gay parody of official reason, of the narrow seriousness of official 'truth' " (11–12).

Players are built up through team folklore into powerful aggressors. The anti-heroes of sports, and the fans who love (and hate) them, come to represent, for most people—especially the feature writers of the sports papers—all that is senseless and destructive in society, thus functioning as folk devils. Set up as visible examples of what is condemned, figures like O. J. Simpson and Mike Irvin come to serve in the popular imagination as images of disorder and evil. Similarly, in Bakhtinian terms, the football stadium and its environs becomes a kind of carnivalesque folk theater for the cultural expression of rage, or the parodic festival of disrespect and misrule, expressed primarily through violent performances and performative utterances, or in misogynistic or racist confrontations, with chants and songs. This code of disorder and misrule, ironically, is always widely accepted.

In terms of aggression, the consistent use of profane language by the football fan dramatizes and enlivens what is being said. Rather than being a limiting factor, this is one of the most successful aspects of the subculture, since it enables the fan to fill his verbal range with a force of meaning and muscularity of style enabling a distinctive and incontrovertible expression of feelings impossible to other, more polite modes of discourse. The aggressive masculinity of these violent and racist chants is often unspecified and enigmatic, but their charge of feeling is usually strong. Such chants have an integrity of form and atmosphere as well as an immediate, concrete confidence, which maintains what Bakhtin refers to in his description of the carnivalesque as a "direct responsiveness" to "living concerns."

These aggressive kinds of football chants serve the purpose of symbolic as well as performative disorder, in which language can serve a ritual purpose, just as the fans' wearing of football helmets and shoulder pads and is symbolic as well as instrumental. In a way, aggressive chants directed at the state of play on the field and occurring in the interactional posturing between rival fans can be interpreted *metonymically*, being recognized as proper parts and adjuncts to real performances of violence. Many of the fans' activities can be understood as symbolic performances in this mode of metonymy: that is, in Bakhtinian terms, words can be regarded as performances of detached elements of sequences of actions which would, if carried through seriously, lead to the injury or death of the rivals.

Studies of the lyrics of black rap singers have demonstrated how such metonymic displays of aggression can serve to establish the rapper's self-identity as part of a community performance. The sense of self-commitment and participation inherent within such localized forms of social organization thereby permits individuals to *reclaim* those elements of their identity that have been abused and misappropriated in other social and cultural contexts. In this way, rappers have reappropriated the white term of abuse "nigger" for individual restatements of black identity. For the football fan, in a similar way, these metonymic forms of aggression and violence allow the reclaiming from fashionable politics of male attributes such as dominant masculinity, the excitement of pursuit and overthrow, and the rediscovery of a forcefully individual male language and space. This is especially important if we remember that a number of football fans are working-class, undereducated, oppressed, and sometimes unemployed.

Quite clearly, the main objective of these stylized male insults seems to be the simultaneous denial of the opponent's masculinity and the reclaiming of the fan's own male space. The most frequently used terms for insulting a rival fan or player are usually words generally associated with sexual functions, such as "motherfucker," "sonofabitch," and so on, usually including such terms of homosexual abuse as "fag" and "queer." Such insulting terms always figure predominantly in the more aggressive songs and jams, and they provide an integral part of the ritual reappropriation of masculinity. Songs and chants like these, incidentally, crop up in virtually all examples of masculine subcultural groups where ritual anthems develop, including all sporting cultures, all-male schools, drinking groups, and, of course, the military.

In his suggestion that carnivalesque laughter occurs in the zone of maximum familiar and crude contact, and sometimes leads to blows, Bakhtin brings an important angle to any discussion of aggression in relation to sports fans. By emphasizing the relation of laughter to violence, Bakhtin emphasizes the *libidinal* nature of laughter and its associations with tension, with bad taste, and with the mocking of death. In effect, Bakhtin foregrounds the nature of laughter as opposing, and yet at the same time connected to, the death instinct. Freud argued that the instinctual aspects of behavior tend to be conservative or regressive, capable of being directed either outwardly or inwardly, just like the sexual instinct, with its object and ego libido. The formulation of Thanatos thus enabled Freud to postulate an instinctual basis for all the hostile, violent, and self-destructive acts that human beings perpetrate

upon each other and themselves. The travesty of the jock jam in particular seems to be instinctual in nature, with many sexual elements,
containing a level of aggression and violence that seems to bespeak the
libidinal associations between laughter and bloodshed.

Clearly, this notion of violence elicits a number of attendant issues,
and the consistently problematic nature of these questions begins to
reveal the limitations of Bakhtin. What can theories of carnival tell us
about the relationship, for example, between the abusive fan and the
object of his abuse? Is the obscene language of jock jams related in any
way to the presence of cheerleaders at many games? A number of these
chants are considered offensive on racist or misogynistic grounds, and it
might be worth speculating whether the kinds of carnivalesque pleasure
attained by one social group can ever compensate in any way for their
violent machismo, and the feelings of oppression and alienation, they
undoubtedly engender in others.

Another limitation of Bakhtin is his tendency toward romantic
populism. In properly reacting to the patrician–pessimistic case about
popular culture, for example, Bakhtin tends to perhaps downplay the
more negative aspects of it, which can sometimes be quite violent and
aggressive. He tends to idealize popular culture in order to rescue it from
the patrician pessimists, and, in doing so, perhaps makes his case less
cogent. What this issue of violence raises, however, is the impossibility,
with a Bakhtinian method, of divorcing the aesthetic from the political
nature of any subculture. It becomes virtually impossible to separate the
behavior of the fans themselves from the ritual or performative significance of that behavior, or the pleasures this behavior involves from the
social and ideological determinants of all subcultures.

Political Conflicts in the Realm of Aesthetics

One of the most interesting of Bakhtin's ideas is his understanding of
the interrelation of aesthetics and politics, and his refusal to ignore
moral and ideological components. Many contemporary critics writing
on Bakhtin, including Linda Hutcheon, have been drawn to precisely
this issue—the ways in which Bakhtin was influenced by Marxism in his
belief that language could not be separated from an intimate connection
with ideology. Bakhtin draws culture into the social and economic
sphere, and suggests that language, a socially constructed system, is itself
a political and material reality. Graham Pechey (1998) writes that
"To understand the radicalism of Bakhtin's thinking is to understand
that in his concepts, the border of the sociopolitical has already been
crossed" (66).

Bakhtinian notions of the carnivalesque, therefore, can help us to understand how subcultures can access social or political conflicts by allowing the parent culture to seem ridiculous and therefore less "venerated," in Bakhtinian terms. In other words, the impulse toward carnival may represent the performance of an otherwise mute and largely unconscious popular resistance to the restrictions and limitations of the parent culture. In a number of ways, it seems, Bakhtin's reading of the carnivalesque helps us to a new and better understanding of the relationship between subculture, performance, and many traditional cultural values, by firstly being predicated over the whole of discourse without exception.

A Bakhtinian reading shows how most fight songs either allude to or contain a series of cultural and countercultural class, race, and other struggles, and their implications of radical and sometimes violent social change present a challenge to institutionalized cultural forms. This revision, moreover, is not limited to the leftward animus of the carnival with its involved collocation of class and cultural struggles. These chants also involve radical right-wing properties and a movement toward the right-wing revision of institutions by, say, displaying frequently unpopular attitudes toward the sexual and political status quo, addressing social inadequacies and hypocrisy in religion and government. It is interesting to consider to what extent both these rightward and leftward properties are bound together in many of the songs and chants. Paradoxically, however, there is a hedonistic element to the fight song as well, in that it often demonstrates a tendency to ignore or disguise the social and political forces responsible for its own shaping.

Bakhtin acknowledges the importance of subculture not only as a fruitful area of study but also as an intrinsic part of lived experience, viewed not from a political or sociological perspective nor as a "lower" branch of culture, but rather as a different (but equally valuable) mythology, sign-system, or aesthetic. He allows for a textual analysis of even the most stigmatized forms of pop culture which, instead of criticizing the simplicity or limitations of such forms, considers the ways in which their particular system of cultural formations presents an alternative version of culture as it is lived. As a result, Bakhtinian notions of the carnivalesque allow us to understand how the uncompromising resistance of the football fan leaves him free to express profanity and confrontation in new, symbolic ways, free to deconstruct social conventions through especially powerful and radical means, and free to unveil the dark face of culture, however obscure and shocking that face may be.

CHAPTER 3

RUMOR, GOSSIP, AND SCANDAL: BARTHES AND TABLOID RHETORIC

In continental Europe, Roland Barthes has been a respected writer for almost forty years, but it is really only since the 1980s that his works have come to wield influence in the United States. His central area of investigation is what he referred to as "semiologie"—the theory of signs, verbal and nonverbal. This is a development of the linguistic theories of Ferdinand de Saussure and Roman Jakobson—theories that also strongly influenced the anthropologist Claude Lévi-Strauss. The work of Roland Barthes, therefore, essentially belongs to that interdisciplinary movement, associated especially with France, generally known as post-structuralism.

In 1947, Barthes began to publish a number of articles on literary criticism that eventually formed the basis of his first book, *Writing Degree Zero* (1953). Subsequent publications included books and articles on Racine, the French "new novel," and semiology, including *Mythologies* (1957), *Elements of Semiology* (1964), *S/Z* (1970) and *The Pleasure of the Text* (1973). In these and other writings, he made a number of radical connections between semiology and cinema, shopping, advertising, fashion, photography, toys, food, margarine, wrestling, and many similar areas of the popular cultural scene.

His central theme could be described as the conventionality of all forms of representation. According to Barthes, bourgeois ideology promotes the view that reading is natural and language transparent; it does so by insisting on regarding the signifier as the natural partner of the signified, thus, in authoritarian manner, repressing all discourse into "meaning." Barthes suggests that one of the hallmarks of avant-garde writing is that it allows the signifiers to generate meaning at will, thereby undermining the censorship of the signified and its repressive insistence on one single "meaning."

The collected *Critical Essays* of 1964 chart the course of Barthes's criticism, from the influences of existentialism and Marxism—reflections on the social situation of literature and the writer's responsibility to history—to a psychoanalytic anthropology, which clearly brought Barthes to his terms of understanding with Claude Lévi-Strauss and Jacques Lacan. Most of the work in these critical essays marks an apparently decisive conversion to structuralism, understood in its strictest sense, whereby literature and social life are regarded as "no more than" languages, to be studied not in their content, but in their structure, as pure relational systems.

In *Elements of Semiology* (1967), Barthes extended his belief that the structuralist method could explain all the sign-systems of human culture. However, in the very same text, he recognized that structuralist discourse *itself* could become the object of explanation through the medium of a second-order language called a "metalanguage." In realizing that any metalanguage could be put in the position of a first-order language and be itself interrogated by another metalanguage, Barthes glimpsed an infinite redress ("aporia"), which destroys the authority of all languages, including metalanguages. This means that, when we read as critics, we can never step outside discourse and adopt a position invulnerable to a subsequent interrogative reading. All discourses, according to Barthes—including critical interpretations—are equally "fictive." None stand apart in the place of "truth."

Barthes was no obfuscating intellectual, and he made his theories widely available in his own lifetime, bringing theoretical debate to the *Times Literary Supplement*, where he invited distinguished English, American, and Continental critics to state their intellectual credos. In his own essays for this magazine, Barthes brusquely denied that criticism is concerned with "truth" in any sense, brilliantly demonstrating that criticism consists not in *discovering* something previously unperceived in the work, but in *covering*, or fitting together, the language of the artist with the language of the critic, and thereby showing that criticism, like logic, is ultimately tautological. All these arguments proved profoundly disconcerting to the orthodox assumptions of literary criticism, in France as elsewhere.

Barthes's intellectual career was distinguished by one major change of stance, signaled by the publication in 1966 of *Criticism and Truth*. Before this, his work had been held together by a profound commitment to the historical nature of discourse. After 1966, however, his writing moved into the mode now associated with Derrida and *Tel Quel*. All of this work is highly relevant to any study of contemporary popular culture. However, the primary texts most relevant to my case in the following chapters are Barthes's earlier work, especially *Mythologies*, and some of his later ideas from *The Pleasure of the Text*, *S/Z*, and *Image-Music-Text*. In the following chapters, I rely particularly on these writings, because it is here that Barthes presents his theory of the "plural text," thus asserting his most effective antidote to conventional hierarchical-based theory. In *Mythologies*, for example, he interprets "the literary" not in terms of French literature, nor "high" culture, nor the avant-garde, nor even as a particular body or sequence of works, but instead recognizes only what he refers to as "semiotic activity"—the complex inscription of traces of a practice: the practice of writing.

As I outlined in chapter 1, in order for Bakhtin's theories to be applied to a wide variety of texts (including orthodoxically ex-canonical texts such as ballads, jokes, folk songs, music, magazines, satire, sport, and so forth), Bakhtin devised the concept of "polyglossia," studying the forces at work within a given literary system in order to reveal the artificial limits and constraints of that system. Almost twenty years later, Barthes extended this thread of Bakhtin's thinking, suggesting in *Mythologies* that "literature" should be regarded not as any particular body of writing or tightly-constructed form, but rather as "semiotic activity." Like Bakhtin before him, Barthes allowed for the application of his semiotic theories to branches of writing traditionally dismissed as subcultural or "non-literary," such as magazines, newspapers, traffic signs, shopping, and song lyrics—and indeed, in *Mythologies*, he wrote about the semiotics of food, fashion, and advertising.

Barthes's version of the literary—or the text—as "semiotic activity" essentially prevents the classification of any type of writing as less worthy of semiotic study than any other. Instead, quite significantly, he provides a separate semiotic context for the critical analysis of each different field of semiotic activity. Thus, although all of Barthes's works are relevant to the following chapters, I rely mainly on those texts in which he refreshes the terms in which we come to study modern cultural forms, recovering for culture new relations, recognizing what had once appeared to be out of the bounds of literary and cultural study—namely, what is *not* literature: our lives.

As Saussure's analysis of language suggests, our perception of the blur of sensation and experience which constitutes our external physical world depends largely upon cultural background, coding, and language. A given culture organizes the world according to given practices, and therefore considers different aspects of the world as pertinent. Practical purposes, decisions about material constraints and so on interact in leading a culture to segment the continuum of its own existence into a given content. Because there is no solid homology between signifier and signified, it is debatable how one corresponds to the other.

The American linguists Edward Sapir and Benjamin Lee Whorf and the British linguist M. A. K. Halliday have suggested that there is a causal relationship between semantic structure and cognition—that is, that language influences thought, that its structure channels our mental experience of the world (and there is plenty of relevant psycho-linguistic research to back this up). Sapir, Whorf, and Halliday argue that between human beings and the world there exist systems of signs that are the product of society. Signs acquire meaning by being structured into codes, the principle code being language. From this perspective, language appears as a self-sufficient system, whose meaning is determined not by the subjective intentions and wishes of its speakers, but rather by the linguistic system as a whole.

In 1938, Bakhtin described language as a system analogous to that of printed texts in a lending library, each of which signifies ceaselessly and several times, and from which the speaker borrows, uses and replaces his or her chosen words. Barthes's interpretation of semiology in *Elements of Semiology* (1967) is very similar to that of Bakhtin's theory of polyglossia, formulated some thirty years earlier. According to Barthes, under each word in modern writing there lies a preexistent "geology," in whose manifold layers the total content of the word is gathered. Thus, Barthes's idea of writing (*écriture*) in *Elements of Semiology* is very similar to Bakhtin's version of writing in *The Dialogic Imagination* as that-which-has-already-been-said. In this sense, according to both theorists, writing is in no way a matter of personal choice, but rises out of the narratives in the writer's unconscious, and goes beyond his or her area of personal control. All writing, according to Barthes in *Elements of Semiology*, is "closed"—not a system of communication, but a route through which passes only "intention to speak."

If linguistic meaning is the product of the codes and conventions of different signifying systems, then it follows that no role can be given to private intentions and individual meanings. In *The Way of Masks*, Claude Lévi-Strauss suggests that by claiming to work independently, the artist is indulging in a fruitful illusion:

> When he thinks that he's expressing himself in a spontaneous fashion, that he does original work, he answers to other past or present, actual or visual creators. Whether aware of it or not, no-one walks the path of creation alone. (18)

In *Mythologies*, Barthes suggests that some areas of our society are very susceptible to the power of coding—for example, the realms of fashion, shopping, architecture, cuisine, and sport. He explains how these codes endow the world with meaning and significance for their users by organizing it into categories and relationships which are not "naturally" present, but which represent the interests, values, and behaviors of human communities. Thus, for example, the difference between "plants" and "weeds" is a semiotic, not a botanical difference—it arises from the tastes and fashions of a gardening culture, and is coded in the vocabulary of our language.

These codes were identified and described by Barthes in 1957 as *mythologies*. Mythologies, according to Barthes, are produced when signs are multiplied so that their "denotable" meaning comes to include (apparently intrinsic) signs of conceptual values. In *Mythologies*, he argues that these myths do the same job as "primitive" myths—they endow the world with conceptual values that originate in language. Thus, these mythologies can be regarded as representations *of* the world, *for* a given culture. Like a map, they work first by segmentation—by partitioning the material continuum of nature and the undifferentiated flux of human thought into slices that answer to the interests of various communities. Just as different types of maps divide and segment the same landscape in different ways according to their intended use, so different mythologies divide up the continuum of physical experience depending on their social, political, and economic purposes.

According to Barthes in *Mythologies*, a myth is the chain of ideas that is associated with a sign, representing a cultural way of making sense of the world. He explains that myths dehistoricize the world so as to disguise the motivated nature of the ideological sign. As a result, most of what we consider "natural" in our culture is actually a form of mythology. Indeed, Barthes believes that all our apparently "natural" "meanings" are in fact a result of cultural conditioning—the result of conceptual frameworks all so familiar as to pass unnoticed. By challenging received opinions and proposing new perspectives, Barthes exposes our usual, habitual ways of explaining the world, and seeks to modify them. He notes how different cultures try to pass off as "natural" elements of the human condition arrangements and practices which are in fact the result of historical forces and interests. By showing how various lifestyles and practices developed, Barthes attempts to demystify the ideology of culture by exposing its unconscious assumptions.

Cultural practices that appear completely "natural," such as wine drinking for the French, for example, are described by Barthes as ideological arrangements and practices to be exposed. He points out in *Mythologies* that, for the French, "to believe in wine is a cultural coercive act" (34), and drinking wine represents a ritual of social integration. Cultures, according to Barthes, make their own norms seem facts of "nature" or "common sense" by generating mythical meanings which seem indomitable, and so even the most "natural" remark about the world depends on a complex series of cultural codes.

Accordingly, Barthes goes on to suggest that the tropes and imagery used in conventional writing in no way indicate the individual writer trying to convey the singularity of his or her own sensations, but rather function as a literary and cultural stamp "placing" a language, much as a label tells us the price of an article. According to *Mythologies*, such cultural systems are ideological, and supported by a social jargon or sociolect through which they identify. In this sense, communication is always a prisoner of the form through which it has to be manifested—codes that become gestures, spectacles in the "theater of language," which fail to retain any trace of individuality.

The Language of News

If there is one single branch of language that we in the West tend to consider more objective and authoritative than any other, it is the "official" language of the news media. Consequently, it is easy to fall into the trap of believing the news to "represent" a series of newsworthy events, whereas it is in fact the *reporting* or *accounting* of selected events. Newspapers do not *report* events that are necessarily meaningful in themselves, but in fact *translate* them into their own meaning-system or scale of values. As individuals, we learn to understand newspapers by actively learning their particular language-system, and as we get used to their codes and conventions, we become "news literate"—able not only to follow the news and recognize its familiar cast of characters and events, but also able to interpret the world at large spontaneously in terms of the codes we have learned from reading newspapers.

In *Language in the News* (1991), Roger Fowler writes:

> We assume that newspapers carry faithful reports of events that happened "out there," in the real world beyond our immediate experience. At a certain level, that is of course a realistic assumption: real events do occur and are reported—a coach crashes on the M1, a postman wins the pools, a cabinet minister resigns. But real events are subject to conventional processes of selection: they are not intrinsically newsworthy, but only become "news" when selected for inclusion in news reports. The vast

> majority of events are not mentioned, and so selection immediately gives
> us a partial view of the world. (10–11)

Clearly, the selection criteria for newsworthiness are constructed by various social factors. For example, the amount of information already available to members of a society may influence the base against which events are considered, with regard to their usualness. Similarly, policies affecting the layout of a newspaper predetermine exactly what *can* be reported about the world. Newspapers include features on sports and fashion, for instance, mainly because other newspapers include features on sports and fashion. Moreover, once some newspaper "ratifies" an event as news, other papers tend to accept that ratification and treat the feature or event as independently newsworthy. Furthermore, newspapers are, by their ephemeral nature, unable to contend with slow-moving, historical cycles and are far better equipped to accommodate rapid, expected change. They are also generally incapable of reporting what seems to be an indeterminate or fluid situation, and may force process on occurrences whose direction is indecisive.

"News" is considered to be "newsworthy" because it is believed to breach our expectations about the world. However, most "news" stories in fact report minor, unexpected developments in the expected continuity of social life and institutions. They *add* to what we already think we know or could predict on the basis of our assumed knowledge about the world. Most newspapers carry only a little "news" anyway. Their single largest amount of space is usually devoted to advertisements, with the rest of their space given over to letters, cartoons, features, editorials, and so on.

All journalists have their own cultural "maps" of the social world by which they "make sense" for their audiences of the ideas that form the basic content of what is "newsworthy" and what is not. Their goals are various. For many journalists, a "good" story is one that holds the reader's attention, and such stories generally involve well-known personalities and are usually "bad" news, often concerning crime. However, certain crimes such as company fraud, which involve members of élite groups, are often ignored altogether, unless the accused is a corporation large enough to attract attention, as in the recent Enron and Worldcom scandals. Where other crimes are concerned, the "presentation of supporting evidence" involves piling fact upon fact in such a way as to *appear* to shed light on a topic, and the judicious use of quotation marks, ostensibly to avoid inaccuracy and bias.

Newspapers have to fill fixed amounts of space allocated to different types of story (e.g., crime, foreign, domestic, society, fashion, and sport), regardless of how much these various types of "news" are happening in the world. At least seventy percent of the material featured every day in most newspapers (including regular surveys of crime figures, letters, editorials, society features, sports results, and so on) is neither spontaneous, nor unexpected: the words most often used to define the popular meaning of "news."

A variety of criteria must be satisfied before an event becomes "newsworthy," and Johann Galting and Mari Ruge, in a famous 1976 study, isolated a series of conditions that have to be fulfilled before an event is selected for nomination. Criteria which "ordinary events" have to satisfy before they become "newsworthy" include the achievement of certain goals in the following areas: frequency (the timespan taken by an event); threshold (the size of an event); meaningfulness (cultural proximity and relevance); consonance (the predictability of, or desire for, such an event); continuity (how long the story will run); composition (the mixture of different kinds of events in the bulletin); reference to élite persons; reference to élite nations; personalization, and negativity. The more of these particular goals an event fulfills, the more "newsworthy" it is considered to be, with the result that "bad news" is especially "newsworthy" because it is unexpected, generally unambiguous, happens quickly, is consonant, and often has a "good threshold."

More significantly, the dominant schematic pattern of newspaper discourse encodes a view of the world which assumes the polarization of groups, conflicts of interest, and the desirability and repression or destruction of "them" (criminals, terrorists, immigrants, rapists, pedophiles, and so on) by the legitimized agents who work on behalf of "us" (the police, "heroes," the government, the senate, the medical profession, and so on). Newspaper discourse generally follows the pattern of an active, authoritative agent (doctors, police, the president) doing something active or violent ("slams," "curbs," "backs," "crushes") to a passive, patient party (Iraquis, children, the homeless, and so on), as in classic "us versus them" headlines like "Judge Slams Rapist," or "President Backs Cuts." In ideological terms, by providing labeling expressions that solidify concepts of "groups," and assigning different semantic roles to the members of these different groups, it becomes possible for the newspaper to discriminate against them, and to assist the practice of distributing power and opportunity unequally among them.

Tabloid Rhetoric

I now want to use the work of Roland Barthes to consider some of the particular mythologies governing the series of codes and conventions by which tabloid journalism functions. In order to do so, however, it is first necessary to refute a number of common assumptions about the discourse of tabloid writing.

Both in Europe and the United States, tabloid newspapers have been mocked and criticized for helping to create a culture of "infotainment," sensationalism, and "checkbook journalism." According to popular assumptions, tabloid newspapers suffer from a lack of seriousness, a deficiency of neutral, thorough and informed coverage of what are deemed "important" issues, and sensationalistic reporting.

Tabloid newspapers are traditionally dismissed as particularly insubstantial examples of popular cultural texts—insubstantial because, presumably, they adopt a simple, repetitive style, a narrow vocabulary, and involve a limited field of subject matter. There are a number of ways in which such criticisms could be refuted. One might claim, for example, that parts of tabloid writing are actually as substantial as traditional literary culture when measured by the same standards. Indeed, there are a variety of alternative aesthetic contexts in which the specific qualities of tabloid journalism (such as repetition, simplicity, clarity, and narrowness of vocabulary) are precisely the reason why other, more traditionally "literary" texts (such as ballads and folk songs) are valued and praised. The repetition of certain phrases, concepts, ideas, and ideological schemas is held to be especially significant and valuable, particularly in ethnographic examples, such as obsessive rhythms, incantatory music, litanies, rites, or Buddhist *nimbutsu*, where excessive repetition— as Barthes explains in *The Pleasure of the Text*—comes to represent loss, the zero of the signified, or Nirvana (41–42).

In the same way, such styles as melodrama and sensation are, in the context of tabloid writing, usually taken to be devaluing and derogatory critical categories. However, in other aesthetic contexts such as opera, melodrama is praised for its ability to move ideological discourse into the domain of the personal, and for its ability to enforce the strongest possible audience identification with character. In fact, the stories that seem to convey the most appeal for the largest number of people are generally the most melodramatic and sensational stories, such as the ones analyzed in this chapter.

It should perhaps be pointed out at this stage that one problem with this kind of "aesthetic" defense is that it ignores the various ways in which tabloid writing regularly discriminates against members of ethnic and social minorities, particularly women, thus assisting the harmful practice of distributing power and opportunity unequally among them, and this is one of the most serious philosophical issues attendant on my position in this book. Rather than getting tied down to such arguments about the question of relative literary values, or becoming obsessed with value judgments that involve moral and ideological components, however, I wish instead to attend mainly to tabloid writing as a substantial and interesting source of aesthetic pleasure.

It is clear that tabloid newspapers do, in some areas, warrant criticism. But what is also clear is that the success of the tabloids is dependent on the entertainment value they provide to the public, and this is one of the many reasons why they are so successful. The sensation and excitement people find in newspapers such as *The National Enquirer* and *The Weekly World News* is a recipe for success in societies that seem to be craving more and more distraction.

In cultures that are highly advanced, technologically, we have as much information available as we can possibly imagine, and so in order to remain profitable, newspapers need to find different kinds of material to present—including gossip, scandal, and rumor. With the globalization of cable television and the vast array of channels available to most people, "serious" news is always available, and the tabloids are a way of getting something different, something other than just "news." It seems clear that the popular press has developed its sensation-seeking paparazzi style because, to a certain extent at least, there is a clear public demand for scandal and gossip. The format and appearance of the tabloids also seems to be very successful. Indeed, over time, "serious" newspapers have taken on a far more "tabloidy" appearance than ever before, including elements of color, and panels showing the highlights of the paper's contents.

A good example of a tabloid newspaper whose rhetorical complexity has been vastly underestimated is the popular British tabloid, *The Sun*. Despite all the criticism directed toward it, *The Sun* is by far the best-selling daily newspaper in Britain, and it has dominated the popular newspaper market for the last twenty years, with a daily readership of over ten million. Ex-editor Larry Lamb noted that the best journalists he worked with on tabloid newspapers like *The Sun* and *The Daily Mirror* could transfer "readily and easily" to the so-called quality newspapers, the so-called unpopular ones. "Many of them did. But the same was not true in reverse" (167).

And yet *The Sun* has always been criticized for its simplicity, and lack of "serious" reporting. According Larry Lamb, in May 1989, Tory M.P. Jonathan Aitken said of *The Sun* that "the reporter's profession has been influenced by a seedy stream of rent boys, pimps, bimbos, spurned lovers, prostitutes and perjurers" (188). Lord Longford, of the Longford Report on Pornography, agreed that *The Sun* and *The News of the World* thrive on "the uninhibited representation of Mr. Rupert Murdoch's particular antipodean blend of erotica" (190). Journalist Bill Grundy commented in 1988 that "Rupert Murdoch's *Sun* makes no attempt to be serious" (136), and Alex Jarrett, head of the Independent Press Corporation, agreed, "I think it's fair to say that *The Sun* is almost wholly trivial" (212). In his book about the newspaper, Lamb quotes Tony Rees, a *Sun* journalist, who claimed:

> I am still amazed at the legion of allegedly intelligent people who wrote about *The Sun* who completely missed its hard political edge. I used to get very angry with all the media peers who could not see past the pretty girls and the bezazz, who did not realize that *The Sun* was a product of enormous complexity. (189)

Ethics and Trivia

Tabloid newspapers are indeed a trivial form of culture—trivial, that is, in the original sense of the word. From the Latin *tri vium*, three roads, the word literally applies to that which is "of the street corner," meaning the everyday, the commonplace, that which is familiar to the round of daily life, and to ordinary people—all of which are true of the tabloid newspaper. But there is another, even older meaning to the word "trivial." A "trivial" art was originally an art belonging in the Ancient Greek *trivium*, originating with Martianus Capella in the early fifth century, followed by Boethius, and his pupil Cassiodorus—as distinct from the mathematically based sciences of the *quadrivium*. The *trivia* consisted of the methodological subjects Grammar, Logic, and Rhetoric, and it is the latter of these in which the tabloid newspaper specializes, in its own consistent and formulaic way.

Rhetoric (from the Greek *rhetor*, "a speaker in the assembly") is the art of using language for persuasion, in writing, speaking, or oratory. Classical theoreticians, such as Quintilian in the *Institutio Oratoria* and Cicero in *De Inventione, De Optimo Genere Oratorum* and *De Oratore*, codified rhetoric very thoroughly. A knowledge and command of it were regarded as essential to the aspiring gentleman of parts. So great, in fact, was the influence of the classical rhetoricians (and, later, of Longinus in the work ascribed to him, *On the Sublime*) that the rhetorical rules for written and oral composition were upheld from Cicero's day well into the nineteenth century, without changing. The five categories of classical rhetoric, in their logical order, were invention, arrangement, style, memory, and delivery, with numerous subdivisions within each category. It was the task of the classical and medieval rhetorician to use language as effectively as possible so as to persuade, a task originally tied to ethics (persuasion of what is true) and literature (the use of language in order to please), and significant for its provision of poetic "devices" (figures and tropes).

The role of the modern-day rhetorician has been assumed not by politicians, whose usually lifeless speeches are heard by only a very small minority of people, nor by the more "substantial" newspapers, whose obligations to an ethic of what is known as "objectivity" rarely allow them to make any discernible efforts toward persuasion. In fact, it seems, the less "substantial" the newspaper is considered to be, the livelier its rhetoric. Indeed, the tabloid newspaper is one of the more powerful and popular rhetoricians in the modern forum, particularly in the places where it is being most sexually and politically conservative.

The Trial of Dr. Jeremy Stupple

On September 16, 1990, the headline story in the British tabloid *The News of the World* referred to allegations against a family doctor, Jeremy Stupple, that he seduced two of his local patients, named on the front page only as "Mrs. A and Mrs. B." Although *The News of the World* had been following this case eagerly for some weeks, at the time this particular issue came out, Dr. Stupple had already been tried and proved innocent by a medical tribunal.

Page two of this issue contained a photograph of the two women dressed in stockings and garter belts. The text read:

> ... these are the two women who until today have only been seen huddled under blankets in between giving evidence against Dr. Jeremy Stupple. They are Mrs. A—Debbie Finlayson—and Mrs. B—Karen Wheeler. A medical hearing cleared Dr. Stupple of having sex with them. Now they tell all.

Pages three and four continued the story by informing us that—

> Blonde Mrs. B—one of the two women who falsely accused G.P. Jeremy Stupple of having sex with them—is a nymphomaniac who has notched up a string of affairs. "I first made love at 13 and haven't stopped since," said ex-convent girl Karen Wheeler, 25.

Later on, we learn that:

> Chairman Sir Robert Kilpatrick said that either monstrous allegations had been made against Dr. Stupple, or he was guilty of monstrous

behaviour. . . . Karen told the hearing that the doctor wore red underpants.

Like most tabloid discourse, this particular story works through a system of connotation, which, as Barthes points out in *S/Z*, can function either syntagmatically (from the cumulative force of a sequence), or paradigmatically (from implied comparison with alternative choices). The last line of this extract is a good example of syntagmatic connotation. "Karen" may well have "told the hearing that the doctor wore red underpants," but the previous sentences have apparently just negated the truth of her utterance by establishing Dr. Stupple's innocence. Mrs. Wheeler's ascribed phrase is strategically placed in the paragraph to confirm the cumulative build-up of what the whole story actually *connotes*, rather than what it *denotes*. If this happened, then that must also have happened. If Mrs. A knows that Dr. Stupple wears red underpants, then she must have been in a position to *see* those underpants, and so on. Such suggestions signify further events in an external "reality" *outside* the text. When *The News of the World*, for example, in a smart marketing move, promises us that Mrs. A and Mrs. B will now "tell all," then presumably, one assumes, they must have something to tell about something that happened in the "real world."

Paradigmatic connotation, according to Barthes in *S/Z*, exploits our expectations of what might have been chosen, in order to compare it with what is there. For example, the "news" photo showing Mrs. A and Mrs. B dressed in bustiers and garter belts connotes "naughty," "kinky" sexuality, and the sex lives it is implied these women lead away from the home and the kitchen, largely because the word "housewife," when used in the *News of the World*, normally suggests an older woman dressed in an apron and rubber gloves working at the kitchen sink. The result of this displacement not only makes Mrs. A and Mrs. B's get-up more significant, but also gives their story a hint of plausibility, even though we have just been told that it is not true.

This hint of plausibility partly explains the popularity of the kitchen and the typing pool as settings for many of the stories in pornographic magazines (see chapter 5). Most working men come into daily contact with a number of housewives and secretaries, which fuels the fantasy with a local sense of specificity and familiarity. This also explains the popularity in such magazines of features like "True Confessions," "Readers' Wives' Tales," "Fact Files," "Kitchen Crumpet," and other such pseudo-feasible "true-life" features. Barthes's suggestion in *The Pleasure of the Text* as to why the reader takes so much interest in the petty details of daily life in the novel (such as references to schedules, habits, meals, lodgings, clothing, and so on) may also explain why the reader of the tabloid newspaper is so fascinated with the incidental details of "human interest" stories, such as the detail of Dr. Stupple's red underpants. In *The Pleasure of the Text*, Barthes suggests that such details might represent "the hallucinatory relish of 'reality,' involving familiar details of a familiar scene, within which the reader can take his [*sic*] place" (53).

Sequences in the story of Mrs. A and Mrs. B (because this is not, by any means, the story of Dr. Stupple) move in a kind of counterpoint. The narrative is, in a word used by Barthes in *Image-Music-Text, fugued*, in that it at once *holds*, and *pulls on* (104). More specifically, when the reader concentrates on one element, such as the cover photograph of Mrs. A and Mrs. B in their stockings and garter belts, they are simultaneously *encouraged* by the narrative structure of the text to use this element to make sense of the opposing one: namely, the "official" establishment of Dr. Stupple's innocence. The reader is simultaneously encouraged by the photograph to implement an alternative reading of the story itself: that Mrs. A and Mrs. B are sexy housewives who always wear stockings and garter belts, and so they *must* have been seduced by Dr. Stupple.

Instead of the more traditional journalistic method of *denotation*, the discourse of the tabloid newspaper works to an alternative system of *connotation*. This system of connotation encodes a particular textual meaning—neither the dictionary meaning, nor the meaning to be found in the grammar in which the text is written, but a meaning that is determined by subtextual elements such as pictures, names, titles, and implications. The system of connotation used in tabloid discourse here carries a double meaning, and therefore corrupts the "purity" of traditional forms of communication. In this example, a deliberate "static" is introduced into the relationship between reader and author, thus turning the communication into a countercommunication.

The aim of the tabloid story is to *maintain* the puzzle and mystery of the story. On the one hand, Mrs. A and Mrs. B promise to "tell all" about the "sin in the surgery," claim "the married G.P. had sex with them," live in a "saucy Sussex new town," have so far only been seen "huddled under blankets," wear stockings and garter belts, Mrs. B is a "nymphomaniac" who told the hearing that the "doctor wore red underpants," and so on. On the other hand, however, the story's structure and sentences cannot help but *unfold* the enigma: a medical hearing "cleared Dr. Stupple of having sex with them," they "falsely" accused the G.P., who was "cleared of misconduct." The interplay between the connotation that Dr. Stupple *did*, in fact, have sex with Mrs. A and Mrs. B, and the denotation that he has been cleared of all charges, enable the tabloid to operate like a kind of rhetorical game, each system referring to reader to the requirements of a certain illusion. Interestingly enough, versions of this story that appeared in British mainstream newspapers like *The Times* and *The Guardian* suggested not only that nothing of any interest happened in Dr. Stupple's surgery, but, more significantly, that the whole story had been set up by the *News of the World*, which apparently paid Wheeler and Finlayson a substantial sum of money for their willing assistance in the charade.

The Perverted Prelate and the Novice Monk

On Friday March 12, 1993, *The Sun's* editorial ("The Sun Says") commented on a story about a Church of England bishop accused of sexually molesting a novice monk over a period of two years. *The Sun* said:

> *UNHOLY ORDERS*
> *Night after sordid night Bishop Peter Ball abused a boy entrusted to his spiritual care.*
>   He committed serious sexual offenses against 17-year-old Neil Todd while reciting Hail Marys and reading the Psalms.
>   But it appears the Church knew all about Ball's nasty habits but chose to turn the other cheek.
>   The police have taken an equally strange view. The perverted prelate will NOT be prosecuted.
>   Strange how the laws of God and the justice of the courts can be so easily brushed aside.
>   *Just as long as you happen to be a Bishop in the Church of England.*

Literary (rather than colloquial) elements of this editorial include the use of repetition ("night after sordid night,") alliteration ("the perverted prelate will NOT be prosecuted"), simplicity, and narrowness of vocabulary. Homosexuality is regarded here as an evil transgression of "the laws of God and the justice of the courts," and this particular example of homosexuality is regarded as being especially wicked since it occurs in the context of a somewhat odd mélange of Bishops, Psalms and Hail Marys (in the Church of England, of all places).

In the full article about the Bishop of Gloucester from the same edition of *The Sun*, ("Rid Us Of This Cancer") we learn that:

> Neil first saw the Bishop of Chichester and was asked to go and see the Bishop of Southwark three days later. He repeated his story and was told his allegations would be relayed "to the highest authority"—which he believed meant the Archbishop of Canterbury.
>
> Neil attempted suicide two days later because Ball still seemed to be working normally. Neil claimed: "Everyone in the Church told me I shouldn't bring in the police because it wouldn't be the best thing to do for me.
>
> "I hate to think how many boys were abused and have to suffer alone because they haven't been able to tell anyone or were pressurised by the Church into keeping silent."

Tabloid stories like this one strongly maintain the tradition of crime broadsheets that proliferated throughout most of the late nineteenth and early twentieth centuries. One of the mythologies of the Victorian crime broadsheet or "penny dreadful" was the notion that there were a number of links between murders, rapes, and crimes of sexual assault. The construction of a mass murderer—or, in the case of the Bishop of Gloucester, a "sex fiend"—helps to sell newspapers, and this concept of a "pervert" or "psychopath" does attract a certain amount of human interest. There are an immense variety of possible stories suggested by crimes of this nature, but there are always certain enduring themes.

In this story, by focusing on themes such as the "naughtiness" of the clergy, the presentation of Church figures as comical "perverts" at the same time possessing indomitable authority, the depiction of all homo-sexuals as pedophiles and so on, not only feeds the political agenda of the law and order lobby, it also creates self-perpetuating material of a similar nature. In this way, rape and sexual abuse function as "human interest" stories rather than as "news." In their book *Sex Crime in the News*, media researchers Soothill and Walby discovered that the two British newspapers that include the most reports of rape and sexual abuse—*The Sun* and *The News of the World*—both belonged to media mogul Rupert Murdoch, and no case of rape is ever covered by both newspapers. Apparently, the possibility of this happening by chance is so remote as to defy calculation, and the authors conclude that this statis-tic explains a marketing strategy whereby *The Sun* and *The News of the World* are, in effect, being sold as one single package. For the habitual tabloid reader therefore, stories of rape and sexual abuse, like the tale of the Bishop of Gloucester, are pornographic titillations, and are treated as such, rather than as "news."

The story of the Bishop of Gloucester is not "news" in the traditional sense because it lacks the social and political context typical of "news." Instead, this is a "human interest" story that portrays a world composed of individuals whose lives are strongly governed by luck, fate, and chance, and who are united in a community that shares common human experiences (sex, birth, death, love, accident, illness). This sympathetic view of life as a lottery fits in very well with the tabloids' compulsive use of competitions, which simultaneously celebrate the virtues of consumption in their glamorous prizes. Human interest stories like this one are always presented in highly personal terms, and they often exploit the minor doings of stars, celebrities, and members of élite groups—such as bishops and doctors—to the full. These stories embody a particular way of seeing the world, a cultural effect that is profoundly ideological in that it disguises the social and political forces that influence the shape of events.

Lovely Lisa

Tabloid newspapers are often at their most powerfully rhetorical where they choose to be the most profoundly conservative, in sexual and political terms. *The Sun*'s best-known and possibly most contentious feature is the Page Three Girl, a phenomenon that provokes regular fulminations of aversion from right-wing family-values campaigners and left-wing feminist factions alike (see figure 3.1).

The image of women in the tabloids is a bone of contention, and has been for the past three decades. The typical image of a "girl" in newspapers like *The Sun* and *The News of the World* is of a person who is "curvy," slim, white, pretty, young, and, more often than not, semi-nude. The Page Three Girl feature began in the 1970s, with a photograph of a "half-dressed Swedish charmer," and continues to the present day even though, since January 2003, the newspaper has been edited by a woman, the 36-year-old former *News of the World* editor, Rebekah Wade.

The most basic and general aim of the Page Three Girl seems to be the minor titillation involved in the display of the top half of a young female torso, thus obviating the awkwardness, for men, of purchasing "top shelf" pornography, coupled with the comforting familiarity of a regular feature. The captions for the Page Three Girl, moreover, have become to many of *The Sun*'s readers a light-hearted and lively characteristic of the newspaper's traditional rhetoric, working to produce in its regular audience feelings of warmth, comfort, and recognition.

Figure 3.1   *Lovely Lisa!* from *The Sun* 8 October 1993

The Sun's Page Three Girl of Friday, October 8, 1993 is Lisa Forward from Essex, who is pictured in front of a blurred, outdoor background (or, at least, a studio simulacra of "outdoors"). Lisa is wearing a pair of tight tartan trousers that she seems to be pulling down slightly at the front, a tartan bow-tie and silver earrings. The caption to this picture reads as follows:

LOVELY LISA'S SCOT THE LOT!
Luscious Lisa Forward lochs just
terrific in this natty pair of tartan
trousers. Lisa, 22, actually hails from Essex—but this outfit's bound to set fellas
dreaming of a Highland fling.

Through a study of this short and highly typical caption in the light of some of the five classical categories of rhetoric, it becomes clear how a seemingly trivial and insubstantial snippet of tabloid language works on a number of linguistic and ideological levels, and contains a series of powerful and sometimes conflicting semiotic implications.

The first of the five categories of classical rhetoric is *inventio*, referring to the discovery of relevant material—as contrasted with "imitation," and with judgment. The nature of the material chosen for Lisa Forward's Page Three caption is highly relevant, not only to what *The Sun*'s readers seem to enjoy, but also to a sexual and ideological status quo. The trappings of the Page Three Girl photograph, for example, generally draw on the images commonly used in pornographic magazines: the model will often be pictured in an office or kitchen, or in sporting outfits, or *al fresco*, like Lovely Lisa, or, most commonly, wearing some kind of uniform such as that of a nurse, librarian, policewoman, airline pilot, secretary, or air stewardess.

The reader of the Page Three feature is also affected by the *inventio* of a series of preconditioned "tabloid codes," which persuade them to set aside conventional ideas of orthodox behavior. These include the notion, for example, that the pants might not be Lisa's own, or that very little of any regular sexual interest happens among secretaries in the typing pool, housewives in the kitchen, or doctors and nurses in the hospital, despite what most pornography would have us believe. Tabloid *inventio* encourages us instead to make sense of the caption according to an alternative system of understanding, where elements such as suggestion and ambiguity are used to replace regular, orthodox readings.

"Lovely Lisa's Scot the Lot!" reiterates some common beliefs of the tabloid's conservative ideology: that young women are chiefly interested in clothes; that "fellas" like to see girls in tight outfits, that "fellas" dream about "luscious" girls; that "luscious" girls like to have "flings," and, on a more basic level perhaps, that Scottish people live in Scotland and wear tartan pants. "Lovely Lisa's Scot the Lot!" corroborates the dominant ideology, wherein potential divergences such as homosexuality, sexual equality, and so on have no place.

The caption to this photograph would have been selected by this issue's Features Editor presumably because it would be seen to appeal equally to all types of *Sun* readers. British tabloid newspapers have been increasingly driven to jettison news in favor of features like Page Three, a process intensified by the changes in style and size initiated by *The Sun* in the late 1960s. "Human interest" features like Page Three originally became popular in tabloid newspapers because they contain a formula by which newspapers could maximize the size of their readership. Although the "human interest" formula tends to ignore things like diversity of political belief among its readers and to de-emphasize politics altogether, it was not, as popular opinion would have it, introduced by unscrupulous proprietors as a deliberate ploy to spread ideological views, but grew, in fact, out of the economic necessity to achieve as large a circulation as possible.

The *dispositio* in classical rhetoric refers to the organization of the material of the *inventio* into sound structural forms. The captions of the Page Three column are always arranged in a literary (rather than a colloquial) pattern that is, to use Mukarovsky's term, *foregrounded*, often to the very edge of self-parody. As Barthes comments in a different context in *Writing Degree Zero*, even a critical reader can be disarmed by the burlesque playfulness of such discourse (52). It is interesting to speculate to what ends *The Sun* employs its idiolectic *dispositio*, particularly in its deployment of rhetorical literary devices. Possibly its use of repetition, alliteration, simplicity, and narrowness of vocabulary allows it to be extremely sexually and politically conservative without disturbing its readers' political assumptions or complacency. In "Lovely Lisa's Scot the Lot!" for example, a "fella" is synonymous with a heterosexual, and Scottishness is defined by its association with lochs, tartan, and Highland flings.

Possibly, this *dispositio* is intended draw attention to the words, when little of importance (in terms of journalistic codes of "newsworthiness") is actually being said. Most probably, however, Page Three's typical *dispositio* has become a light-hearted and lively characteristic of *The Sun*'s traditional rhetoric, which works to create patterns of familiarity and homeliness for the regular reader.

One very noticeable feature of the *elecutio* of Page Three is that much of the text is technically aesthetic, habitually employing structural patterns that are characteristic of literary, rather than colloquial, discourse. In particular, this column regularly employs a careful selection of rhetorical tools implemented by classical writers and orators like Cicero and Quintilian to enhance the persuasive powers of their tracts and speeches.

The sentences accompanying "Lovely Lisa's Scot the Lot!," for example, both adopt parallel and rhythmic phrase structures. The first is divided equally by a clear caesura ("Luscious Lisa lochs just terrific / in this natty pair of tartan trousers"), while the second and somewhat longer sentence is split into regular antithetical halves by the use of a dash ("Lisa, 22, actually hails from Essex /—but this outfit's bound to set fellas dreaming of a Highland Fling"). Alliteration is ubiquitous ("Lovely Lisa,"

"Luscious Lisa," "Terrific . . . natty tartan trousers," "fellas . . . fling,") and assonance gives the sentences a facility and ease ("actually . . . Essex," "outfit's bound," "set fellas").

The caption also involves a series of saucy puns, again highly typical of tabloid discourse, including "Scot the lot," and "lochs just terrific," and the association of "bound" with the double entendre, or *dilogy*, of "fling." The apposite hyphenation of Essex is also part of the joke, as is Lisa's improbably aptronymic last name. Deliberate misspelling is another habitual stylistic tic, especially *aphaeresis* (the suppression of an unstressed syllable, as in "Scot," from the Greek meaning "a taking away"), and *apocope* (the dropping of letters from the end of the word, as in "fellas").

The "natty" tight tartan trousers that Lisa is pulling down at the front represent a kind of synecdoche in which the general idea substituted (female sexuality) is considerably removed from the particular detail, which in this case is Scottish tartan. This in itself is a fine example of *morology* (from the Greek, meaning "foolish speech") a rhetorical device comprising the use of deliberate nonsense or foolishness for effect. And the threefold repetition of the name "Lisa" in the caption takes the rhetorical form of *epanalepsis* (from the Greek for "a taking up again") a figure of speech that involves the repetition of a word, or words, after other words have come between them.

The implication of the first sentence—that Lisa, who has "Scot the lot," is wearing the tartan pants because she comes from Scotland—is refuted by the second, where we are told that Lisa, in fact hails from Essex. This is a popular rhetorical technique known as *epanothorsis* (Greek "setting straight again") a figure of speech in which something said is corrected or commented on. The whole passage itself, finally, is an interesting example of *exergasia* (from the Latin for "amplification") a rhetorical device whereby a number of figures of speech amplify a point and embellish a passage.

The two other branches of classical rhetoric, *memory* and *delivery*, are not really relevant here, since their concern is the oral rather than the written word, being involved with guidance on how to memorize speeches, and elaboration of the techniques used when actually making speeches. Nor are they wholly irrelevant, however—tabloid discourse demonstrates an obsession with rhythms, balanced phrase structures, antithesis, alliteration, and assonance, which is highly suggestive of the spoken word. It contains, in other words, *clausula*, a form of prose rhythm invented by Greek orators as punctuation for oral delivery. The prose of Page Three is typically scannable, in the same way that verse is; for example, tabloid discourse has developed the technique of concluding sentences and periods with regular cadences.

The Pleasure of the Text

The rhetoric of the tabloid newspaper evokes a mood that aspires to be at times playful and relaxed, at times saucy and cheeky, at times winsome and fresh. It is a rhetoric designed, above all, to give pleasure to the reader. But pleasure of what nature, and at what price? It is difficult to define exactly the quality of pleasure to be gained from reading tabloids, which clearly depends to a large extent on the individual reader. For the reader who wants complete escapism, tabloid newspapers provide thrilling, titillating images and captions that either ignore or disguise the political forces responsible for their shaping—sexual conservatism, anti-feminism, homophobia, heterosexuality, xenophobia, racism, and so on.

The majority of readers, however, read tabloid newspapers in order to find out what is "happening" in the world around them, and to immerse themselves in the tabloid's way of seeing things—a way of reading that may, ultimately, be quite damaging. For example, many tabloid stories both arouse desire for the forbidden (young girls in tight pants, extra-marital sex, sexy outfits, "flings," and so on) while, simultaneously, the majority of the tabloid's regular "news" stories seem geared toward warning readers what will happen to them if they try to act out such desires in reality (shame, court cases, AIDS, scandal, prison, and so on). Some might argue that this psychological double-bind (pleasure-frustration) is resolved, for readers of the tabloids, only by recourse to legitimate (i.e. consumer) objects of desire. Such a reading would interpret the new cars, fridge freezers, satellite dishes and so on advertised as competition prizes as the legitimate consumer substitutes for the pleasures suggested by such sex-romp scandals.[1]

By sketching a series of similarities between classical rhetoric and the discourse of tabloid newspapers, I neither make lofty claims about tabloids, nor advocate their politics. Indeed, as this analysis has in part suggested, by exercising very real and very damaging powers of persuasion, tabloid discourse not only oppresses every under-represented minority group, it also obscures diversity and specificity, lumping all racial, ethnic, and minority groups together, especially in its belittling and trivialization of women. What I would argue, quite simply, however, is that in the context of their own aesthetics and meaning systems, tabloid newspapers have been gravely misrepresented and underestimated as products of great substance and complexity.

CHAPTER 4

"THE LAST STOP OF DESIRE": ROLAND BARTHES GOES SHOPPING

> Each separate counter was a showplace of dazzling interest and attraction. She could not help feeling the claim of each trinket and valuable upon her personally and yet she did not stop. There was nothing which she did not long to own. The dainty slippers and stockings, the delicately-frilled skirts and petticoats, the laces, the ribbons, hair-combs, purses, all touched her with individual desire . . .
>
> Theodore Dreiser *Sister Carrie* (1900)

In this chapter, I try to understand some of the pleasures of shopping in relation to Barthes's ideas in *S/Z* and *The Pleasure of the Text* about plural texts, looking at the activity of shopping as a particular example of a plural text. I pay attention to the history of shopping, the relationship between women and shopping, shopping as an example of *process* as opposed to *stasis*, and the idea of the active shopper as a blank space or empty page to be "filled in." This also involves consideration of the activity of shopping as a network of analogies and affiliations, especially in relation to Barthes's version of the plural text in *S/Z* as a collocation of ideological values, ontologies, and statements. In this light, it seems also important to consider some of Barthes's ideas about encratic language, and to think about the language of advertising and consumption and the typography of the marketplace as examples of encratic language—that is, language produced and spread under the protection of power. Finally, I want to discuss the activity of shopping as a text of *jouissance*. While many writers and critics confess to feelings of angst and paranoia in the marketplace, others, particularly the Futurist writers of the early twentieth century, have regarded shopping as a magical, sublime homecoming to a rediscovered self. It is in this context that I want to examine a particular shopping center, London's Covent Garden Market, and to think closely about the relationship between

Covent Garden, ideas about packaging and surface, and the many kinds of pleasures that are located in the popular process of consumption.

Shopping as Plural Text

The activity of shopping provides a good example of what Barthes refers to in *S/Z* as a "plural" (or "starred") text (13–15). A plural text is the kind of text to which we can gain access by several entrances, none of which can be authoritatively declared as the main one. To put it another way, the plural text is the kind of text that can never be seen in its entirety as the *whole* text. Indeed, this kind of text is separated from all the conventional image-systems of language inasmuch as it is itself composed by all that is barely tolerated or bluntly rejected as insignificant, ex-canonical, and so on by conventional theories of literature and linguistics.

In *The Pleasure of the Text*, Barthes suggests that it is not necessary for a nonlinguistic text to be analyzed linguistically, or in terms of one single method that is given priority over all others. As an alternative to analyzing the text in terms of language, Barthes suggests an analysis of the text in question in terms of the semiotic substance of several kinds of criticism (psychological, psychoanalytical, thematic, historical, structural), and it will then be up to each kind of criticism to come into play, to make its voice heard, which is the hearing of one of the voices in the text. Thus, a plural text such as the process of shopping, which includes a vast range of commodities on display and an ongoing process of movement and renewal, may be reread several times in order for each voice to make its appearance.

Shopping and History

One entrance to the plural text of shopping might be through an analysis of the modern social history of shopping, since everything is, of course, historical. Nonetheless, although much work has been undertaken on the history of shopping, there is a very obvious and important way in which the concept of history is not especially relevant to this activity. Because chain-store shopping centers and chain-stores within shopping malls are virtually identical, and because cycles in trade names, chain-store development and advertising appear to have virtually no historical memory, discussions of the role of the shopping center in national life often lack a historical dimension. As with many forms of popular culture, the very application of historically "proven" and allegedly universal concepts such as permanency and durability seem to have little relevance to recent disposable phenomena.

On the other hand, it could be logically argued that this appearance of "having no past" is deceptive, and all part of the illusion that consumer capitalism wants to generate. Mall-scale shopping could only be said to be historically irrelevant if one buys the illusion, and the ideology underpinning the illusion, of consumer culture. Shopping does of course have a history (see Wolfgang Haug's *Critique of Commodity Aesthetics*, Walter Benjamin's writings on the Arcades Project and so on), the same way that everything has a history. While I intend to suggest that for a variety of reasons history has in fact little relevance in a discussion of the contemporary shopping environment and consumer culture, history *does* seem highly relevant in the discussion of specifically located shopping arcades.

A number of fashionable "reconstructed" European shopping centers, for example, not only share important structural similarities with American-style mall complexes, but function at the same time as historical landmarks with a unique and specific cultural and architectural history. The tradition of such loci is closely linked to the development of the "spectacle of goods" arcade and the history of authenticity and artifice, as found in works such as Thomas Richards's *The Commodity Culture of Victorian England*, and Anne Freiberg's *Window Shopping: Cinema and the Postmodern*.

Women and Shopping

A perhaps more appropriate way in which we could gain access to the plural text of shopping is through an examination of the relationship between women and shopping, since it is women who are primarily defined as consumers. This is a line of reasoning many feminist writers on shopping have taken up. For instance, in her book on the department store entitled *Just Looking*, Rachel Bowlby shows how the psychoanalytic construction of femininity is very much like that of shopping, in that during the process of shopping, the female shopper is being looked at (or "consumed"), while looking at and consuming commodities for sale, and playing games with her own self-image. According to Bowlby, therefore, a woman's sense of self is of a self that is consumed, while she herself is consuming:

> As the proportion of goods sold in stores rather than produced at home increased, it was women, rather than men, who tended to have the job of

purchasing them . . . The superfluous, frivolous association of some of the new commodities, and the establishment of convenient stores that were both enticing and respectable, made shopping itself a new feminine leisure activity. (27)

On both counts then—the increase in women's purchasing responsibilities and the potential for some of these for extra excursions into luxury—it follows that the organized effort of "producers" to sell to "consumers" does to a large measure take the form of a masculine appeal to women. Moreover, to "go shopping" originally invoked a relative emancipation in women's active roles as consumers. Given the traditional confinement of women to the domestic sphere, shopping did at least originally take women out of the house to urban areas formerly out of bounds, as labor-saving equipment made housework more manageable. In today's increasingly complex society, the traditional association between women and the marketplace has become more subtly codified. Even within marriage, women are more often financially independent and in control of a separate income. But this discourse of power and independence may be illusory. The relation of female "spending power" to female "earning power" is a critical question, as Anne Frieberg has acknowledged:

Shopping is more than a perceptual mode involving the empowered choices of the consumer, it—quite simply, quite materially—requires money. A credit-card economy may encourage the fantasy of *virtual* "spending power," but this imaginary diversion has a price. Veblen read female consumption as a "vicarious" sign of a husband's or father's wealth. Today's female consumer may be enacting a postmodern version of an equally "vicarious" empowerment; instead of deferring payment to husband or father, she defers payment to the bank. (118)

However, while it would be of course wrong to suggest that men and women are equal in terms of their engagement in shopping behavior, more men now participate in shopping as a leisure-time activity (particularly in shopping malls) than would ever have dreamed of doing so in the past: gender roles are altering in line with the economics of consumer capitalism. A number of consumer specialists have asserted that men increasingly participate in the shopping chores, and that are therefore involved in brand choice in a way that has not really been considered to date. Consequently, the standard, statistical, market-based analysis of the relationship between women and shopping has become a somewhat outmoded and possibly even invalid route of access to this shifting plural text.

Shopping as Process

According to Barthes, another typical condition of the plural text is that it involves a condition of process, movement, change, and indecision without ever stopping for a static appraisal of connotation and meaning. " 'Text' dissolves ideologies and power systems; the plural codes are forces which 'take over' like imperial invaders" (21), writes Barthes in *S/Z*. It is no coincidence that today's shopping malls and arcades with their escalators, mirrors, fountains, stage-lights, glass fronts, and rocket-ship lifts stand as the ultimate symbols of shopping's future, since they proclaim that it is in the city itself that everything happens first. The relevance and effect of this illusion of futurity seems to depend on a constant schema of updating, reconstruction, movement, making, and *process* rather than the finished product. Or, to put it another way, consumption has come to represent movement, activity, and energy being injected into a state of torpor.

In *S/Z*, Barthes analyzes the consumer as an empty page to be written on and filled in by the experience of the plural text, which represents a kind of homecoming. Barthes characterizes the consumer of the plural text in *S/Z* as a prescribed vessel filled with a series of codes, words and languages to which certain aspects of the text correspond, a view which depends on regarding the consumer of the text not as a unique individual, but as a "plurality of other texts, of codes which are infinite or, more precisely, lost (whose origin is lost)" (10). Where Bakhtin thirty years earlier regarded the text as a composition of heteroglottal layers and codes, Barthes in 1973 considered not only the text but also the *reader* or *consumer* of that text as similarly composed of a series of heteroglottal layers and codes. He suggests that all texts depend on a series of codes we have in us anyway, and to which we respond. Indeed, the visual consumption of the commodity is so much a part of our daily landscape that we do not consciously notice how meanings are inscribed in our acts of consumption.

This version of the shopper as an empty page to be inscribed or "filled up" by the plural text of the shopping process is devastatingly summed up by a photo by Barbara Kruger (called "Untitled"), which presents that abstraction of self and reality in consumer society with the image of a white hand with thumb and forefingers grasping a red credit-card-like item whose motto reads "I shop therefore I am." Kruger's photo captures the double nature of commodity fetishism as it informs both self and activity. The reduction of *being* to *consumption* coincides with the encratic mixture of articles and advertisements in the abstraction of the shopping process, exactly as it does, incidentally, in today's style magazines (see chapter 1).

Part of the mysticism of the shopping process is that the crowds, density, shop-fronts, glass windows, and colorful displays seem to provide a network of correspondences and connections whose synthetic quality is somehow both emotive and functional at the same time. In his book *Soft City*, for example, Jonathan Raban notes that each London shop is a symbolic reinterpretation of an ideology, or a lifestyle. Raban's typical Londoner locates a form of artistic beauty in the very idea of all the frenetic movement that consumer culture demands.

Collage and Consumption

No one feature of this living urban collage seems so *alive*, or offers such a catalogue of variety in its signs and synecdoches, as the shopping mall. In this, the very heart of consumer culture, the collage of the city springs most actively to life—a process analyzed most subtly by Walter Benjamin in his work on the Arcades project and in his seminal discussion of collage in "The Work of Art in the Age of Mechanical Reproduction" (1969).

In David Harvey's book *The Condition of Postmodernity*, Harvey seeks to correct many of the ahistorical, implicitly reactionary tendencies manifested in a lot of much earlier postmodern theory of consumer culture. In doing so, he analyzes the expansion of media and communication in the West that appears to have resulted in the seeming compression and reduction of space and time. One aspect of this phenomenon, for example, is the "internationalization" of products on display in the market place or shopping mall: gourmet French cheeses are now widely sold across America, and a British-style pub will often offer German, American, Australian, and Dutch beers on tap. Every market is now much more international than it was twenty years ago. Harvey explains that ". . . spaces of very different worlds seem to collapse on each other, much as the world's commodities are assembled in the supermarket and all manner of subcultures get juxtaposed in the contemporary city" (46).

This vast network of analogies and affinities which characterizes the plural text of the shopping center has been the inspiration for a great deal of modernist art, especially pop art and the art of the Futurists, whose appropriation of the language of advertising and consumption was an attempt to eliminate distinctions between high and mass, between the culture of the gallery and the culture of the market place. For example, Futurist writer Filippo Marinetti testified that his art drew its vitality from modern city life, with its "ever-vaster gradation of analogies" and "ever-deeper and more solid affinities, however remote" (85). For Jonathan Raban, consumer culture is a "labyrinth," honey-combed with such diverse networks of social interaction, oriented to such diverse goals, that it becomes a maniacal scrapbook filled with colorful entries that have no relation to each other (40). In other words, the modern shopping mall obliterates the distinction between construction work and sculpture, between collage and modern life, between process (or, in shopping, trans-action) and finished product (or purchased commodity).

David Harvey describes consumer culture as "an encyclopedia of styles" in which a sense of hierarchy or even homogeneity is in the process of dissolution (301), and in which distinctions between high and mass, or market place and gallery, are finally obliterated. For Harvey, the shopping center is far more than the shops past which Raban's latter-day *flâneur* walks; it is a complex synecdoche for levels of wealth and lifestyles. Harvey describes these advertisement hoardings, window displays and shop fronts as examples of "miniature escape fantasies" ("this, it seems, is how we are destined to live, as split person-alities in which the private life is disturbed by the promise of escape routes to another reality") (301).

Like Marinetti's discovery of a panoply of secret connections, affini-ties and analogies in the heart of the city, Harvey's vision of modern culture as composed of video screens, television commercials and print advertisements also draws on the notion of modern consumer culture as a kind of collage or catalogue. And at the 1986 Trade Fair in Milan—the city, incidentally, which inspired Marinetti's first Futurist Manifesto—Umberto Eco observes how consumer goods "become a series of pure connotative signs, at an emotional fever pitch, each commodity losing its concrete individuality to become so many acts in an anthem to progress, a hymn to the abundance and happiness of consumption and production" (184). No wonder, then, that the plural text of shopping, with all its neon light displays, video screens and elec-tric billboards, its vast area of commercial naming and lettering, should be located by a number of recent artists and writers as the center of "reality" for the postmodern self.

Encratic Semiotics

In *Mythologies* of 1957, Barthes analyzes how the language of money and commodities has become an all-encompassing signifying system, the very texture of everyday forms of ideology. He shows how advertising images, which constitute a large proportion of the shopping mall's collage, are themselves a collocation of ideological values, ontologies, and statements. In *Mythologies*, he deconstructs the ideology behind the semiology of consumerism—that is, the signs in shop window displays (described by Marinetti in 1912 as "those beautiful, brand new toys for thoughtful families" [85]), analyzing the bizarre, often dramatic advertising scenarios featuring soap powders and cleaning liquids that liberate the freshness by symbolically "killing" the enemy: dirt.

The typography of the shopping center, advertising and the market-place are full of examples of what Barthes in *Mythologies* refers to as *encratic* language—that is, language produced and consumed under the protection of power, the language of repetition. Much later on, in *The Pleasure of the Text* of 1973, he refers to "the bastard form of mass culture" as "humiliated repetition: content, ideological schema, the blurring of contradictions—these are repeated, but the superficial forms are varied: always new books, new programs, new films, new items, but always the same meaning" (40).

Earlier, Barthes had implied that all official institutions of language repeat: "schools, sports, advertising, pop songs, news and so on all continually repeat the same structure / meaning / words" (40), suggest-ing that the stereotype is a political fact, a major figure of ideology (incidentally, Peter Handke's play *Kaspar* is all about this). Elsewhere, however, Barthes refers to "the bliss of the stereotype," suggesting that repetition can be responsible for creating happiness, and he refers to a number of ethnographic examples such as totemic chanting rites and Buddhist *nembutsu*. Perhaps a more interesting example would be the pleasure a baby feels in repetitive games (the *fort/da* scenario described by Freud in "Beyond the Pleasure Principle"). Here, however, there is quite clearly a darker side to the repetition ritual, in that the child is seeking to abreact a painful memory. Freud went on to use this style of trauma to develop his concept of the *Wiederholunszwang*, or "compulsion to repeat," in relation to the death drive.

Shopping Center Typographics

One of the most interesting and important ways in which shopping center aesthetics have been acknowledged is in the appropriation of typography as collage, first utilized by the Futurist movement in the early twentieth century. The Futurists tended to transcribe their poems, *diktats* and political manifestos in experimental texts that frequently involved huge gaps, spaces, omissions, the absence of punctuation, large letters for extra emphasis, small letters in the same words as capitals confused with subheadings and numbered lists, vertical printing, onomatopoeic devices, white spaces and attacks on syntax. As Maria Drudi Gombillo and Teresa Fiori explain, Futurist artists deployed the typography of the early capitalist market place (see figures 4.1–4.4):

> The placard, the sandwich man, the poster, the sign, the advertisement, the leaflet . . . Since advertising's intentions were thought to be vulgar, its means could be untraditional. Garishness of color, juxtapositions of boldwood typefaces, the use of illustrative arts . . . the mix of fonts, the stridency of exclamation points and under-scorings, all these could be employed . . . to advertise a product and sell it. Typographic novelty began . . . in the marketplace, catching the accelerated pace of an urban culture. (294–295)

Later, Andy Warhol and the pop artists of the 1950s and 1960s were to utilize the slogans, jingles, graphics, typography, and commercial style

Figure 4.1   Filippo Ton Maso Marinetti, "CHAIRrrrrrrR" (© 2004 Artists Rights Society (ARS), New York/SIAE, Rome)

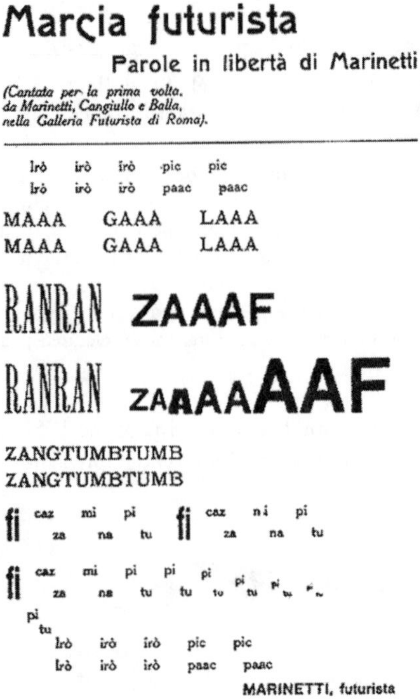

Marcia futurista

Parole in libertà di Marinetti

(Cantata per la prima volta, da Marinetti, Cangiullo e Balla, nella Galleria Futurista di Roma).

```
Irò    irò    irò   ·pic   pic
Irò    irò    irò   paac   paac

MAAA   GAAA   LAAA
MAAA   GAAA   LAAA
```

RANRAN **ZAAAF**

RANRAN zaₐₐₐₐ**AAF**

ZANGTUMBTUMB
ZANGTUMBTUMB

fi caz mi pi   fi caz ni pi
    za na tu   za na tu

fi caz mi pi pi pi pi ti ti ti
    za na tu tu tu tu tu tu tu
pi
  tu
    Irò   irò   irò   pic   pic
    Irò   irò   irò   paac paac

MARINETTI, futurista

Figure 4.2 Filippo Ton Maso Marinetti "Marcia Futurista" (© 2004 Artists Rights Society (ARS), New York/SIAE, Rome)

of consumer culture within their art, constructing collages that depicted an active, functional *mélange* of consumer information. On another level, Barthes notes in *The Pleasure of the Text* that encratic language is essentially designed to keep ". . . desire within the configurations of those upon whom it acts" (40). The encratic language of advertising and consumption and the typography of the marketplace both help to compose the configurations of desire encoded by the plural text of shopping, as the work of the Futurists and pop artists seems also to point out.

Consumption: Pleasures and Displeasures

There are, of course, a number of reasons *why* people shop. For those who are interested only in "hanging out" in shopping malls, viewing the different range of goods on offer, playing games with their own

Figure 4.3   Carlo Carra "Patriotic Celebration" (© 2004 Artists Rights Society (ARS), New York/SIAE, Rome)

self-image and so on, then the pleasure to be obtained from shopping is possibly similar to that which Barthes in *The Pleasure of the Text* describes as *jouissance*, something he advocated, and believed to be inherently good. At other times, however, the shopper is liable to get caught in the psychological double-bind enforced by the encratic language of the mall. Many of those who are interested in the shopping process have pointed out that encratic language creates this psychological double-bind by promising to put back by means of signifiers (in other words, *commodities*) what has been taken away from the consumer at the level of the signified (i.e., his or her sense of potency). Walter Benjamin's *Passagen-Werk*, translated into English as *Arcades Project*, bears directly on this paradox. As Benjamin helpfully points out, this simultaneous arousal of desire and frustration occurs via commodity fetishism. This pleasure–frustration paradox *appears* to be resolved by recourse to these legitimate, or consumer,

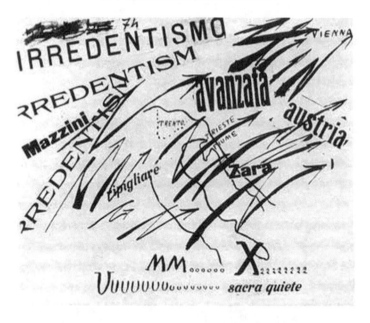

Figure 4.4   Filippo Ton Maso Marinetti, "Words-in-Freedom" (© 2004 Artists Rights Society (ARS), New York/SIAE, Rome)

objects of desire, but the lack of subjectivity intimated in the pleasure of the immediate purpose can only ever be fleetingly achieved.

Many people who write about shopping are critical of the fantasy utopia it offers people. Susan Willis, for example, in *A Primer for Daily Life*, sees the forces of capitalism as conspiratorial because they put profits before individuals. She points out that the distinction Nancy Reagan's anti-drug campaign told us to make between good and bad commodities was a hypocritical one:

> Commodity culture tells us to say yes to everything. To question a commodity strikes at [its] fundamental logic. The admonition against drugs precludes the possibility of raising awkward questions about all the other commodities defined as acceptable. We need not question what we consume. The supermarket has done this for us. (146)

Willis regards consumption as false consciousness, a sign of commodity fetishism. She characterizes the attractive image of commodities as capital in its hypothetical utopian form, promoting the false notion of democratized consumption. She argues that the ideology of consumer society "defines atomization as strength, while bonding with others to facilitate social reproduction is a sure sign of weakness and insufficiency" (176).

This negative appraisal of shopping and commodity consumption is perhaps the most understandable reaction to the awe and intimidation engendered by the confusion and alienation of the shopping mall. A George Romero film, *Dawn of the Dead*, features zombies taking over a shopping center, a scenario depicting the worst fears of culture critics like Clement Greenberg who have long envisaged the will-less, soul-less masses as zombie-like beings possessed by the alienating imperative to consume. Incidentally, *Dawn of the Dead* became a midnight favorite in cinemas in shopping malls all over America—a cult symptomatic of the masses reveling in the very demise of the culture they appear most frequently to support.

Possibilities for commodity consumption in the European market-place meet the tremendous scale promised by the American mall only in a few special locations. These distinct shopping environments are rather more varied and diverse, in history and structure, than their U.S. counterparts and equivalents. Harrods and Selfridges in London, for instance, are both "department store" environments, somewhat different from the more "self-conscious," constructed environments of outdoor or indoor shopping centers or enclosed shopping malls, and the historically constructed shopping environment of Covent Garden. As Meaghan Morris eloquently demonstrates, each shopping locus looks and operates according to its own particular dynamic, and while similarities exist in terms of the display of goods and so on, shopping behavior in each style of location probably differs.

Nevertheless, any consumer activity on this kind of vast scale must inevitably produce a sense of the individual's alienation and confusion, a feeling of the self being lost in a conspiratorial fever of newness and the consumer gaze. The concrete reality of the mass and the sameness of the crowd in such places often result in what is described as a sense of lack, of loss, of absence. In Florida, as Kroker, Kroker and Cook point out, most of the shopping centers—the aptly named Mercado, for example—possess the layout of a "charming village setting" while containing, of course, the produce of an international marketplace. Kroker, Kroker and Cook observe that there are so many of these pseudo-village "settings," Floridians have no need for villages or towns, or even cities. The whole of south Florida, they point out, has become a series of suburbs, euphemistically dubbed "metropolitan complexes," connected by freeways (110). This alienation of the individual by the urban landscape has been the cause of great outrage. "The more you consume," wrote the Situationiste Internationale on the walls of Paris during the anarchic anti-fascist uprisings of 1968, "the less you live."

Shopping and the Futurists

The Futurist writers affirmed nascent industrial capitalism in nearly industrialized Milan. They loved its violence and *hard* qualities, not the *soft* values of consumer capitalism analyzed by Jonathan Raban, among others (and therefore it might be unwise to leap *too* easily from Cendrars and the Futurists to the modern shopping mall). The Futurist writers of the early twentieth century regarded the process of shopping as a sublime, magical, and mysterious homecoming to a rediscovered self. Shopping centers and malls like the *grands magasins* of Paris (such as Les Halles and the Arcades project) and Berlin were referred to memorably by Blaise Cendrars in 1909 as "the last stop of desire" (68). That mystical fascination with power that Marinetti identified in the huge, collage-like catalogue of connections and affinities of the modern city seems to be realized today in the modern shopping mall, with its glass and chrome architecture, waterfalls, and neon shop-front displays—the kind of metalized, mechanized, commercial art to which Cendrars and Marinetti were looking forward in 1913 and 1909, respectively.

It is clear from Marinetti's and Carra's Futurist manifestos that the Futurist movement regarded the popular type of artificial, surface-oriented architecture as not only aesthetically beautiful but somehow spiritually transcendent, its dependence on consumption a metaphysical ideal. The Futurists eliminated traditional distinctions between the consumer-based, money-making designs of mass consumer culture and the autonomous, noncommercial artifacts of high art. In a piece from 1927, for example, Kasimir Malevich referred to advertising as poetry, as "the flower of contemporary life." "It represents," he claimed, "the warmest signs of the vigor of today's men—indeed, one of the seven wonders of the world" (19). To Blaise Cendrars, the typology of the market place was a sign of life, of warm friendliness and beauty:

> Have you ever thought about the sadness that streets, squares, stations, subways, first-class hotels, dance-halls, movies, dining cars, highways, nature would all exhibit without luminous signboards, without the false blandishments of loudspeakers, and imagine the sadness and monotony of meals and wine without polychrome labels and fancy menus? (103)

In the earlier writings of Cendrars and Malevich, there are often implications that visions of the shopping center or *grand magasin* are almost transcendental ones, in which the process of shopping and consumption is an august transaction mystically asserting the presence of the human soul.

To agree with Cendrars and Malevich in welcoming the activity of shopping-culture is not necessarily to discount the criticism of Susan Willis and other writers of the fantasy utopia this shopping culture offers people. Of course, the moral and ideological components of shopping pleasures cannot at any point be disentangled from the social and economic determinants of shopping itself, since this is, after all, a preeminently economic process. Keeping the criticism of Willis and others in mind, I wish to suggest simply that there are different ways of approaching the text of shopping. To agree with Blaise Cendrars and Kasimir Malevich is to interpret what some believe to be the inescapable alienation of the self in consumer culture as a joyful loss of subjectivity similar to what Barthes describes in *The Pleasure of the Text* as *jouissance*. Both lines of argument, moreover, reach the same conclusion—that this lack of subjectivity can never be sustained, and that shopping is, in the end, inherently unsatisfactory.

In *The Pleasure of the Text*, Barthes describes the plural text as an object or body ("corpus") whose function is the production of pleasure for the consumer. The text, writes Barthes, should be "an object of pleasure" related to the "pleasures of life." Indeed, Barthes theorized the *jouissance* of the consumer as one of the major internal codes and conventions governing the text. He points out in *The Pleasure of the Text* that the idea of *jouissance* has seldom been included in studies of literature or cultural studies, and is generally set aside as irrelevant to textual criticism. Barthes's promotion of hedonism—of looking for *enjoyment* in the text, of "the pleasure of the text"—is therefore, in his view, a very radical step. The task of analyzing the process of shopping thus partly involves exploring the common sensations, perceptions, and emotional states aroused by it, which can often be blissful and delirious, as well as, in the case of Willis and a number of Marxist writers, wary and critical.

In her essay "Things to do with Shopping Centers," Meaghan Morris points out that the shopping center form itself (as a building consecrated to the perpetual present of consumption and "nowness") is one of the few new building types of our time. Like department stores before them (and which they now usually contain), shopping centers are often described as palaces of dreams, halls of mirrors, galleries of illusion, and so on. This rhetoric is, of course, related to the vision of the shopping center as Eden or paradise, as a mirror to utopian desire.

These Edenic allegories of consumption in general, and of shopping centers in particular, can be found in a number of modern reveries on the subject of shopping culture. Meaghan Morris, for example, is interested in what differentiates particular shopping centers from one another, looking at how they produce and maintain what architectural writer Neville Quarry calls "a unique sense of place"—that is, a mythology or an identity. Morris points out that, despite their constant aura of change and "nowness," shopping centers *can* produce a sense of place for economic, come-hither reasons, and that this *dual* quality is very much part of the shopping center's strategies of appeal, "seductiveness," and also of its management of change. "The stirring tension between the massive stability of the center and the continually shifting population of shoppers is one of the things that people who like shopping centers really love about shopping centers" (46), writes Morris. The contemporary urban shopper is naturally accustomed to the spectatorship demanded of the consumption process because this kind of spectatorship is almost directly paralleled by cinematic forms, including television and video. Anne Frieberg's work on cinema and the postmodern prudently analyzes the correlation between cinematic spectatorship and the construction of the consumer gaze.

The shopping process can be described as a text of *jouissance* because it can be, for some, a passionate experience, an expressive act. If we willingly choose to buy into the ideology of consumer capitalism often denounced as "false consciousness," we can begin to understand how an accepted form of social democracy is embedded in the ever-present, neon-lit, time-free shopping mall or the ubiquitous invitations of the busy urban street. If we buy into the ideology of consumer capitalism, we all trade equally in the culture, and success in today's society is the affirmation of the individual as a maximizer of consumption. What typifies the writing of French theorists like Guy Debord and Jean Baudrillard is the antic image of a society in which consumers and commodities seem to circulate freely and endlessly in a fantastic democracy of consumption.

Of course, there are many different ways of shopping, and different shoppers can attain *jouissance* from the process of shopping in a variety of different forms. For some, *jouissance* is attained simply from being present in the shopping mall itself, with its glass and chrome architecture, its colored signs, its spectacular galleries and gigantic luxurious halls. For other shoppers, the moment of *jouissance* is the actual moment of purchase, when the carefully wrapped item transfers ownership and becomes part of the shopper's daily life and cultural meanings. And then for shoppers like Nicole Diver in F. Scott Fitzgerald's *Tender is the Night*, shopping is a kind of mystical, transcendent rite of passage affirming a mystical process of regeneration and renewal:

> Nicole bought from a great list that ran to two pages, and bought the things in the shop windows besides. . . . She bought a dozen bathing suits, a rubber alligator, a traveling chess set of gold and ivory. . . . As the whole system swayed and thundered onward, it lent a feverish bloom . . . to [her] wholesale buying . . . (123)

And it is in this particular context—of shopping as a text of *jouissance*—that I want to read London's Covent Garden Market, and the many shopping-pleasures it contains.

Covent Garden Market

Covent Garden is centrally located, with its own subway station, and has developed into one of London's most popular attractions, not only for tourists, but also for a divergent population of locals and other Londoners. Unlike most shopping centers in the United States, the market is a traditional local landmark with a unique "history", which was constructed into a public shopping area in 1830 by the architect Charles Fowler, and originally designed as a produce market. The area's name recalls the ancient convent garden tended by the monks of Westminster Abbey. When he abolished the monasteries in 1536, Henry VIII bestowed this land upon John Russell, the first Earl of Bedford. The Earl's descendants developed it into a fashionable *piazza* in the seventeenth century, and retain a financial interest in the area until this day. Covent Garden was abandoned as a produce market in 1974, and subsequently restored by London County Council to its 1880 appearance, with the additional creation of two sunken courts, significantly increasing the leaseable area available. The historic pattern of structures and streets was left undisturbed, leaving the original urban fabric intact. It is this (artificial) historical "authenticity" that links Covent Garden to traditional shopping loci such as the "spectacle of goods" arcade analyzed by Benjamin.

These two internal sunken courts now both house Italian restaurants, while the walkways framing the courts are lined with small, upmarket, expensive shops specializing in designer clothes and uniquely English items directed mainly at the wealthier class of tourists—hand-carved pipes, leathers, rugs, woolen garments, home décor, and so on. On either side of these walkways, further on, wider stone passageways contain mainly small boutiques, also very expensive, selling mostly women's clothing and lingerie, with a couple of men's specialist tailors and outfitters, and one or two Italian terrace restaurants.

To the right of these passages is the main courtyard, a large, wider, open area, still under cover, surrounded by less exclusive, more reasonably priced wholefood cafés, fast-food takeout stands and shops selling CDs, videos, DVDs, gifts, and clothes similar to those on sale in Carnaby Street and elsewhere. Moving further east toward the subway station, this courtyard gives out on to a large cluster of cheap, crowded, piled-up stalls selling mainly music, posters, and postcards, and still further to the east are four rows of open market stalls, catering mainly to a youthful population of shoppers. These stalls sell such items as shoes, clothes, hats, and bags, all very similar to the ones on sale elsewhere in London, at Camden Market, for example. All over this area are other, smaller stalls and sometimes just salesmen, often of dubious legality, selling tourist items, postcards, watches, electronic goods, and so on. It is this area of the market that is perhaps the most "authentic," since Charles Fowler's 1880 produce market would have been a similar cluster of haphazard, transient one-man stalls and booths, rather than the smoothly designed shop-fronts and stone walkways of the reconstructed indoor market areas.

Inside the indoor market itself, the walkways and staircases are all stone, framed by iron railings, balconies, black gaslights, authentic-looking signs detailing the names of streets and so forth, and plants in large wooden urns, and wheelbarrows. The main courtyard is surrounded by wide cloister-like stone archways—broken up by seats, plants, wheelbarrows, signs, and the seats and tables of open-air eating areas— and a high, raftered, pigeon-filled roof covers the whole structure. The open market outside is also cobbled, but contains no wheelbarrows, walkways, or plant pots.

Covent Garden has a relaxed, informal, and interesting setting. The large public space in the main courtyard is regularly populated, especially on Saturdays, by entertainers, music, magic acts, mime, buskers, theater, circus acts, performing animals, and so on. The activity of shopping in this area is thereby transformed into a form of entertainment where the shopper population is relaxed and therefore, at least according to the theories of Covent Garden's designers, in the mood for spending money—an example of a supposedly "natural," irrational urge in consumers, which is in fact the result of a rigorously rational entrepreneurial scheme.

This relaxed, holiday atmosphere is greatly enhanced by the numerous enjoyable, non-shopping activities "surrounding" the shopping area, which characterize the uniqueness of the environment. A number of stage-design shops, moss-covered "artisan's studios" and lively pubs skirt the shopping environment "proper," including the notorious Lamb and Flag—the pub where poet John Dryden was attacked and nearly murdered by an angry mob opposed to his writings. Other diversions in the area include the Cabaret Mechanical Theatre in the Punch and Judy pub, the Bow Street Magistrates Court, and the site of the booksellers' home where Boswell first met Dr. Johnson in 1763.

The only part of the original *piazza* to survive is architect Inigo Jones's St. Paul's Church, known as the "actors' church," because a number of famous actors and artists are entombed within its interior. Flanking the reconstructed square itself—perhaps best known for its appearance in the movie set of *My Fair Lady* (see figure 4.5)—are the Theatre Royal and the Royal Opera House, both of which date from the nineteenth century. The former, embellished with an impressive portico and a long, blue colonnade, has been the site of three attempted regicides. The latter, one of the world's few great opera houses, is also the home of the Royal Ballet.

These fascinating and illustrious places are not associated with the shopping activities within the market directly, but play particular roles in determining the consumer behaviors encountered in Covent Garden. For example, much like the lively space of the main courtyard which serves to entertain shoppers with its traveling mime and magic acts, St. Paul's Church and the Theater Royal provide additional diversionary activities for shoppers. The presence of these diversions may help to explain the consumer behavior of the non-shoppers or onlookers who decide to visit the shopping areas after visiting the Mechanical Theatre or the Royal Opera House, with no particular purchases in mind. The reconstructed market's pivotal location in the center of many unusual non-shopping activities is another studied meditation on the part of its crafty designers.

Covent Garden is also a place for urban socialization, and certain areas have been specifically designed for shoppers to stroll, meet, sit down, relax, and chat—promenades, balconies, terraces, indoor gardens, plazas, and so on. The areas around the open market and the edge of the main courtyard are populated especially by young people, both shopping and just hanging out—listening to music, trying on clothes, leafing through racks of posters, skateboarding, smoking, sitting around, watching each other, enjoying themselves without necessarily

Figure 4.5   Covent Garden Market as the backdrop for a scene from *My Fair Lady* (George Cukor, 1964)

spending any money. There is also a variety of eating opportunities available to satisfy the divergent shopper population at different times of the day or night. The shopper can choose among terrace restaurants, indoor cafes, stand-up counters, fast-food takeout stands, the food hall in the main courtyard (an international array of takeaway food stalls surrounding a large communal area of tables and chairs), or, in the open market outside, hot-dog and hamburger vans.

The interior and exterior spaces of Covent Garden are related, and the public pedestrian areas of the market are integrated with existing street and pavement systems outside through the use of multiple large entrances. These exterior spaces, such as the cloister-like structures surrounding the main court, flow freely into buildings and are joined with interior pedestrian areas. The indoor market has a number of plaza-level connections and subtle level changes whose connections to the main cobbled courtyard are enhanced by the visual transparency of the stone archways—it is possible to see in and out of all of the buildings all of the time, creating a sense of spaciousness, air, light, and freedom. This continuity of pedestrian spaces, moreover, means that the shopper circulation is smooth, varied, and effortless, and the fact that there are so many different routes to choose from means that every shopper's visit is, each time, somewhat unique. This is partly what Jonathan Raban is referring to when he describes the city as "soft, amenable to the dazzling and libidinous variety of dreams, interpretations" (15), a place where individuals can "be themselves" while performing a multiplicity of roles.

In a way, the shops lining the internal walls of Covent Garden represent an example of what Guy Debord referred to forcefully in the 1960s as *le spectacle de la marchandise*. The items displayed in these shop windows are in no sense basic items bought for definite needs, but are there mainly to be looked at, for visual fascination and for the remarkable sight of things not to be found at home. A couple of these shops present extremely visual window displays of paintings and holograms, as though the display itself existed simply to provide the shopper with entertainment, with no obligation to buy, or even, for that matter to enter the store. Moreover, the contemplation (rather than the purchase) of such luxuries is no longer—as in the early days of the market—a prerogative of the aristocracy, since they are there to be seen by everybody.

For those critical of this notion of democratized consumption, Covent Garden is somewhat unique since it also offers an alternate perspective. In contrast to the costly and exclusive items displayed in the chic and beguiling indoor shops, the open market outside contains ranks of simple, small, individual stalls, manned personally by the stall-holders and their families, with no advertising, window displays, or publicity except for the occasional shouted encouragement. Here, the shopper can browse through racks of used clothing, exchange books and music, stop and chat or haggle over the price of goods for sale. Obviously, this is quite a different form of shopping from that which takes place within the internal quarters of the market, and the juxtaposition of the two Covent Garden "markets" in this fashion—surely anticipated by the market's designers—creates an authentic feeling of democratized consumption. Thus, the shopper without much money to spend, or with no specific purchase in mind, can browse and window-shop in the internal structures of the market, before spending money in the open market outside—a kind of shopping that almost everybody can afford.

It should be pointed out, however, that this fusion of shopping-cultures is fairly rare, and in fact unseen in suburban chain-store malls in Europe and the United States, with rare exceptions, such as Les Halles in Paris. And while the *feeling* of democratized consumption may be an authentic and liberating one, and while many people certainly visit both areas of the market, the same *consumers* do not tend to move from one market to the other. The goods outside are not lower-priced substitutes for the goods inside, so those shoppers who consume at the outdoor market are most likely obliged to do so out of economic necessity, not because of a better deal outside, nor because of personal choice. Quite clearly, window shopping in the interior mall engenders a kind of desire that cannot be fulfilled by the act of shopping in the outdoor market, and so the sense of democratized consumption evoked by the market's relaxed mix of activity is obviously an illusion.

And this is only one of the many different ways in which the internal "reconstructed" Covent Garden market is essentially *not real*. It is a theatri-cal representation of a nostalgic image of a kind of street life that no longer exists, in most of the United Kingdom, at least. When Covent Garden was reopened in June 1980, extensive press coverage described it as "London's first permanent late-night shopping centre," an "upmarket shopping leisure development," "London's new historic shopping experience," and so on. And although the 1980 reconstruction was ostensibly built to the market's original design with great concern for authenticity—the wheel-barrows are the original flowersellers' carts, for example—all the "gaslights" are actually electric and "glazed" in plastic, the modern sprinkler system for extinguishing fires is fairly naked, and the cash-registers in the upmarket, air-conditioned stores are all of the newest kind, meaning that several are linked by telephone to credit-card company hotlines. Critic Peter York feels that there is something about it that reminds him of Disneyland in Florida. "Covent Garden is a good example of the commercially success-ful consolidation of enthusiasms," writes York, "—the enthusiasms of the aesthetics of design types who create, endorse and consume today's . . . art-directed worlds where everything is designed" (10).

To those who regard the shopping spree as an example of bewitchment by the false consciousness of consumerism, there is a clear connection between this fake theatrical representation of a nostalgic urban street life, and the emphasis in the shopping mall (and in other aspects of popular culture) on the process of surface and packaging. This emphasis also seems to be related in some way to the concept of *newness*. In her book *Consuming Passions*, Judith Williamson suggests that the power of the purchase—taking home a new thing, the anticipation of unwrapping—seems to drink up the desire for something new (13). Susan Willis points out that commodities in the shopping mall are always introduced as "new," and forever afterward must repeat this moment of "newness," even if it is the same old laundry detergent, packaged in a new box and endowed with a new "fresh scent." "Newness ensures that consumption will be a unique experience, will in fact have the power to compensate loss" (47), writes Willis. Jean Baudrillard agrees. "Everyone has to be up-to-date and recycle himself annually, monthly, seasonally, in his clothes, his things, his car," he writes in *Idées*. "If he doesn't, he's not a true citizen of consumer society" (46).

Possibly, part of the success of the refurbished Covent Garden is due to this constant illusion of "newness," even, ironically, in the "new" repackaging of history, and the market's unique blend of historical "authenticity" with an "upmarket shopping leisure experience." I would add, however, that in the case of Covent Garden, it is not necessary for the shopper to be "bewitched" by this theatrical representation of urban street life and the false consciousness it is supposed to produce. It would easily be possible to spend a pleasant day in Covent Garden spending no money whatsoever—clearly, large numbers of people often do. Even for the visitor who *does* spend money, however, it is possible to consciously *join in* this celebration of artifice, packaging and plastic, of image rather than reality, of *shopping*, rather than what is bought.

Indeed, rather than being alienated by it, most of the shoppers and young visitors to Covent Garden seem happy to participate *in their own ways* in the pseudo-authentic "shopping event" that is being offered, where, instead of just consumer goods, stores ostensibly retail festivity, relaxation, and magical shopping "adventures." Many of the young shoppers and visitors use the spaces available in the outside market and the main courtyard in their own ways, to use its spaces for their own form of revelry and pleasure—for meeting, chatting, listening to music, and so on. Other visitors use the spaces Covent Garden offers in order to make their living, either by putting on a circus act, dance, or magic show, or else setting up their own (illegal) stalls, making use of the vast and diverse shopper population as both audience and customers.

Covent Garden's emphasis on *appearance*, on *seeming* rather than *being*, on *gesture* rather than *substance*, gives pleasure to any shopper or visitor able to participate in this game, or to reinterpret it in their own way, without necessarily falling victim to a capitalist charade. Sometimes the most recognizable commodity—that is, what is seen as wholly "artificial"—is somehow freer of past associations, and therefore more capable of giving access to alternative meanings.

For those shoppers and visitors to Covent Garden interested in re-interpreting its spaces for their own uses and their own meanings, for those who are interested in hanging out in shopping malls, viewing the different range of goods on offer, trying on different clothes, playing games with their own self-image, and so on, then the pleasure to be obtained from shopping and its related activities is hedonistic, and similar to that of *jouissance*, something Barthes advocates, and believes to be inherently propitious. For most other shoppers, however, the psychological double-bind enforced by the encratic language of consumption can be avoided neither by recourse to legitimate (consumer) objects of desire, nor by the pleasures of packaging and "newness." For these shoppers, *jouissance* is achieved only fleetingly, in the moment of purchase, as the shopper discovers an anodynic joy in abandonment to the imperative to consume.

CHAPTER 5

BLUEPRINTS AND BODIES: LACAN AND THE PORNOGRAPHIC IMAGINATION

In his most influential and perhaps most important work, *The Four Fundamental Concepts of Psychoanalysis* (transcribed and translated from a series of seminars at the *Ecole Practique des Hauts Etudes* in Paris in 1973), the French psychoanalyst Jacques Lacan professed to be a Freudian, and left it up to his students and followers, as he put it, to be Lacanians. Indeed, Lacan's psychoanalytic theories are rooted in Freudian psychoanalysis, though they have evolved and developed over the years to meet the (often practical) requirements of a constant reformulation of psychoanalytic theory.

According to Freud in his 1906 work *Three Essays on the Theory of Sexuality*, during the earliest phases of infanthood, the libidinal drives have no definite sexual object, but play around the various erotogenic zones of the body (oral, anal, and phallic). Before gender and identity are established, there is only the rule of the "pleasure principle." The "reality principle" eventually supervenes in the form of the father who threatens the child's Oedipal desire for the mother with the punishment of "castration." The repression of desire makes it possible for the male child to identify with the place of the father, and with a "masculine" role (the Oedipal voyage of the female is apparently much less straightforward). This phase introduces morality and religion, symbolized as "patriarchal law," and induces the development of a "superego" in the child. However, this repressed desire does not go away and remains in the unconscious, thus producing a radically *split* subject. Indeed, according to Freud, this force of desire *is* the unconscious.

The work of Jacques Lacan basically involves a reinterpretation and a critique of classical Freudianism in the light of structuralist and post-structuralist theories. It is virtually impossible to provide a dilution or summation of Lacan's basic ideas, first because Lacan himself preferred that many of his texts be left entirely unglossed on the grounds that any comment would prejudice their effective operation. More significantly, however, Lacan strongly objected to the "secularization" of psychoanalysis, particularly in the United States, and pointed out that the whole aim of analysis is to reveal to us that which we do not know—or, more appositely perhaps, to show us that we do not know even that which we think we know. The unconscious, according to Lacan, is virtually unknowable, and to provide a summation of his ideas seems to be quite alien to the nature of his work, which is particularly resistant to interpretation of this static, "logical" kind.

Lacan is not interested in an instinctual unconscious that precedes language. In *The Four Fundamental Concepts of Psychoanalysis*, he maintains not only that the unconscious is structured like a language, but that it is itself the *product* of language—that the unconscious is structured *through* language, and its entry into culture. According to the Lacanian model, the human subject is formed, as Bakhtin and Barthes had both previously suggested, in relations with the world outside, which are constructed developmentally in the process of language acquisition. Lacan's arguments are complex, and it is not my project to recite them at any length here. I simply wish to signal the argument linking together human subjectivity, the unconscious, and language.

Freud devised his theories of the unconscious in the face of a pre-Saussurean linguistics, anticipating the claims of structuralism and poststructuralism. In order to understand Lacanian theory, it needs to be placed in the context of Saussure's concepts of signifier and signified, of which Lacan makes so much use. In Saussure, the signifier has a stable relationship with the signified. Lacan, on the other hand, points to the sliding of the signifier over the continuum from which the signifier is selected. Lacan also makes a distinction between what he refers to as the Imaginary and the Symbolic, where the Imaginary corresponds to a state in which there is no clear distinction between subject and objects, and no central self exists to set object apart from subject, as is possible in the realm of the Symbolic.

"The Mirror Stage" is a paper of Lacan's from 1949, a revision of an earlier version. In this paper, he develops Freud's concept of the ego as it appears in his essay "On Narcissism" of 1914, and rejects the later Freudian theories that appeared in *The Ego and the Id* of 1923. Lacan suggests that in the prelinguistic "mirror phase," the child, from within this Imaginary state of being, starts to project a certain unity into the fragmented self-image in a mirror (this does not have to be an actual mirror); he or she produces a "fictional" ideal, an "ego." However, the

Imaginary tendency continues even after the formation of the ego, because the myth of a unified selfhood depends on this ability to identify with objects in the world as "others." Nevertheless, the child must also learn to differentiate itself from others if it is to become a subject in its own right. With the father's prohibition, the child is thrown headlong into the "symbolic" world of differences (male/female, father/son, present/absent and so on). The "phallus" (not the penis, but its "symbol") is, in Lacan's system, the privileged signifier.

Lacan posits a gap (*glissage*, or *béance*) between the Symbolic order (the post-mirror phase self, which contains such concepts as character, personality, ego) and the Imaginary order (the realm of non-differentiation, of collective identity), represented metaphorically in language as the division between signifier and signified. According to Lacan, this gap represents the division between psychic maturity, when the ego is fully developed, and the time coeval with the mirror phase, of a magical and animistic mode of thought, when the young child has no sense of difference between self and Other, between subject and object worlds.

Lacanian theory seems a highly appropriate form of semiotic analysis to apply to film, mainly because of the similarities between mirror and screen, not least of which being the fact that the darkness of the cinema allows us to temporarily "forget" external reality and retreat to an earlier mode of being, when we were absorbed in the surrounding world, with no separate sense of "self."

Pornographic Fictions

Pornography is a thriving industry. The last twenty years, in the West, have witnessed a massive increase in the production and consumption of pornographic magazines, DVDs, videos, books, and websites. This increase has been attributed to a combination of two factors: first, evidence has suggested that fear of AIDS has caused some people to reduce their sexual activity, and this has created the need for further pornographic stimulation, both between regular partners, and for solo use. Second, the increased availability of home VCR and DVD players has caused a home viewing revolution, and the production of porn on digital video is rapidly expanding, especially since VHS tapes and DVDs can now be discreetly purchased or downloaded from the Internet. Even without taking the Internet into account, there are four times as many "adult" stores in the United States as there are Macdonald's restaurants, and, on a world scale, reliable surveys show there are thousands of pornographic magazine titles being published at any one time.

Porn movies made in the United States in the first "permissive" wave of the 1960s fell into two distinct categories—hardcore, and softcore. Softcore porn films depict sexual activity consisting mainly of nude display and simulated sex. In hardcore, the cast participates in actual sexual activity. Hardcore also includes "specialist" material—that is, sadomasochism, scatology, pedophilia, and so on, some of which is illegal, but still widely available, both on the Internet and "under the counter" in adult sex shops. The increase in the production and consumption of hardcore material since the 1970s and 1980s has led to the growth of a large body of academic analysis and critique concerning pornographic fictions. Just as the post-1970s "new moralism" and liberation of access to "adult" material led to the rapid expansion of the porn industry, so has the liberal access to sexual material led to more ease and comfort in discussions about the development and discovery of all different types of sexuality.

The area of pornography is a hotly debated field, both in terms of the law and in terms of morality, but nowhere is the issue more stormily contested than within academic feminism. Edging my way tentatively through this spectrum of conflicting assertions, I believe that a space can be reached where Lacanian theory may be transformed into a feminist pro-pornography critique that is, at the same time, fully cognizant of the limitations of Lacan. To reach this space, I feel it is important to begin by questioning some of the major anti-porn tenets on which much feminist criticism of the genre is based.

The kinds of analysis from which my critique in this chapter develops include the debates about pornography in *Screen*, the work of Linda Williams, and also the arguments about "active" reading—especially with regard to romance fiction, as in the work of Janice Radway—some of which I investigate in more detail.

Much feminist anti-porn material fails for me because it seems to include an unquestioning assumption of what is and is not pornography, particularly in distinction from feminist "erotica," such as the work of lesbian director Candida Royalle, for example. Pornography and erotic literature are often discussed together but in contrast, as though one defined the other. According to feminist writer Gloria Steinem:

> By identifying *pornography* (literally, "writing about female slavery") as the preaching of woman hatred, and thus quite different from *erotica*, with its connotation of love and mutuality, there was also the beginning of an understanding that pornography is a major way in which violence and dominance are taught and legitimized that is as socially harmful as Nazi literature is to Jews or Klan literature to blacks. (223)

Sexual activity of various kinds has been represented in the art of most cultures since their first emergence. In Greek pottery and Indian temples, for example, sex in its different forms appears as just one subject among many, and it is only in post-feminist Western cultures that a distinction has come to be made between two supposedly different kinds of sexual representation—the pornographic and the erotic. This, surely, needs questioning. I would suggest that the idea of a more fluid movement between pornography and erotica, between mainstream and marginalized, and between masculine and feminine, might be rather more helpful than Steinem's fixed binary oppositions in thinking about the nature of pornography.

The same question also applies to the depictions of sexual activity in porn (and the United States law courts have been debating this issue for years). Do explicit representations of the body cease to be pornographic when they are acknowledged to be "high art" or "great literature" (as in the work of Robert Mapplethorpe, Henry Miller, D. M. Thomas, or Andy Warhol)? Why are more self-conscious "adult" movies by female directors like Candida Royalle, Nina Hartley, and Annabel Chong invariably described not as pornography but as *erotica*? Susanne Kappeler (1987) suggests that art and literature in western society enjoy a status comparable to that of religion in earlier societies, requiring an *a priori* belief in the power of culture, and an unshakable faith in its embodiment of a self-evident good. It is as a result of this faith that works of "art" are apparently beyond criticism, and beyond change (27).

Pornography is generally identified and dismissed by feminist anti-porn critics as a branch of fiction that has no characters, no plot, and— it is often assumed—"nothing but sex." But this, again, seems to be too easy a dismissal. At what point does character cease to become character? At what point does sexual activity cease to be, or to have, plot? Kappeler argues that the definition or categorization of something as *literary* relies crucially—and, in the end, circularly—on its successful association with something else already classed as *literary* (an author, a director, a producer), as in the case of Nagisa Oshima's *Empire of the Senses* (1976) or Pier Paolo Pasolini's *Salo* (1975), both of which include depictions of unusual sexual activities, and both of which are highly valued "classics" from critically celebrated directors.

Such a critique, however, begs the tricky question of finding a definition of pornography that is more useful than the standard dictionary citation of "obscenity in literature and film," with the accompanying legal definition of "obscenity" as that which can be proved to "deprave and corrupt." Despite its quasi-Biblical terminology, this definition is perhaps nearest to the mark in its thrust: pornography can best be described as material that has a certain, usually physical effect on the reader or audience. A more specific definition might refer to "fictive or visual material primarily designed to sexually stimulate a certain audience"—which, in the majority of cases, tends to be almost exclusively male. I take this as my working definition of pornographic material for the purposes of this chapter. Others, however, might argue—and quite plausibly—that surely what constitutes the *pornographic* is not an intrinsic quality of the material itself, but has more to do with the consumer's attitude and thoughts about the material, the polysemy of images, the issues of use, audience, meaning-making, and so on. In this case, the nature of the pornographic becomes virtually impossible to define.

Pornography and Psychoanalysis

It seems clear to me that a psychoanalytic perspective for the study of porn is far more fruitful and rewarding than most other branches of feminist criticism. The problem with a lot of anti-porn theory is that, when applied to material with a specific meaning and a special set of conventions, it analyzes not what the material means to the people who are using it, but what it means to feminist anti-porn theorists, who often assume they know more about the material than the actual users and consumers who are familiar with it. How do feminist anti-porn arguments apply to lesbian porn, for example?

The route to a workable feminist pro-pornography argument must, I feel, pass through the realm of psychoanalysis because, in their explanation of sexual difference, psychoanalytic readings present relevant problems for feminist and other theorists attempting to understand the politics of gender and personal life. Psychoanalytic insights can be especially useful in analyzing the meaning of fantasy, and can illuminate some of the contradictory pleasure and discomfort that most women, and probably men, feel in regard to pornography.

Freudian psychoanalysis, however, has many feminist opponents. Freud has often been accused of producing phallocentric theories—of taking man as the norm, and woman as what is different from man. His depiction in *Three Essays on the Theory of Sexuality* (1905) as woman being characterized not simply by *difference*, but also by *lack*, has provoked a number of attacks from feminist critics. Freud's opponents are concerned to right the balance and develop theories that explain how men and women in their psycho-sexuality are equal but different. Other critics argue that Freud, particularly in "On Female Sexuality" (1931) and "The Psychological Consequences of the Anatomical Distinction Between the Sexes" (1925), among other works, draws solid lines to communicate what we now know is only a blurred merging. Juliet Mitchell (2000) considers Freudian "myths" as merely symbolic stories set up to explain other stories, and so the Freudian search for laws becomes the search simply for lines to sort out the blurred picture. Other feminist theorists see the Freudian account of female sexuality as cutting women off from an early and untroubled psychic unity (a primordial state of fusion with the mother) that feminists should, according to scholars such as Luce Irigaray (1985), seek to restore.

Probably the most significant potential for a feminist pro-pornography argument can be found in Lacan's rereading of Freud. The French Lacanian school of thought has, in fact, been heavily influential in academic feminism, while the Freudian object-relations schools of thought have been absorbed into a more popular form of feminist theory. Lacanian theory is a relevant analyzing practice to apply to pornographic fictions because it provides vast potential for the analysis of nonwritten media such as film and video, because it has particular reference to the body, and because of the numerous associations between the "mirror phase" and the scopic gaze of the voyeur.

In a number of ways, however, Lacan and feminism make uneasy bedfellows, and the major issue in creating a feminist pro-pornography argument is to find a theoretical space able to contain both Lacanian elements and feminist theory without losing the power of either. The difficulty lies in transforming Lacanian psychoanalysis into a feminist theory fully cognizant of the limitations of Lacan, and it is the need to resolve this difficulty that directs my analysis of each text in this chapter.

Of course, there are a number of very significant distinctions between written and visual porn. While most people would agree that visual images provide the most direct kind of sexual stimulant, the written word is able to direct our attention more precisely to specific details and images without the background distractions of setting, soundtrack, and so on. Written porn is therefore more particularized and circumstantial in terms of its details, which can be a very useful quality in helping us understand its power.

Most porn magazines regularly feature "true-life" stories, either in the guise of well-researched "case histories" or "readers' letters." Possibly, this touch of authenticity adds a dash of spice to the stories, perhaps helping readers to imagine them and identify with them. Or perhaps this situating of the story within a familiar world helps to accommodate it into other fantasies perpetrated by the media (about housewives, secretaries, office staff, nurses, teenagers, babysitters, and so on), thus matching the sexual fantasies already well-installed in the (male) reader's image-reservoir. Idiomatic differences in speech are fairly common, especially in the regular scenario involving a macho, working-class man—often a home repair or delivery man—and a more refined, prim, puritanical-seeming woman. In such cases, the man's aggressive and masculine sexuality is contrasted with the woman's refinement, which is often quickly "broken down," so that she becomes the typical "whore in the bedroom" of so many male clichés. These erotic narratives are highly archetypal, often incorporating the themes of guilt, shame, and transgression. What appears to makes them exciting to the reader is the notion that the sex that they involve is "naughty," "dirty," "shameful," or just plain "wrong"—not morally or ethically "wrong," but "wrong" nonetheless.

Shame and Sexuality

The connection often made in the West between shame and sexuality has always been difficult to understand, and it became especially problematic after the publication of the first Kinsey report in 1948, which had an enormous impact on people's attitude toward sex. It was Kinsey's insistence that sexual activity be separated from traditional moral judgments that led to the new sexual freedoms of the 1960s, and encouraged the enjoyment of so-called "guilt-free" sex. And yet the notion of "guilt-free" sex, as these erotic narratives suggest, is a compli-cated one, and it brings up a rather difficult question: can sex in western culture ever be really "guilt-free"? And, more significantly perhaps, do we ever really *want* it to be?

Specifically, the "guilt" in these erotic narratives seems to stem from the disparity between how a person is in their everyday life, and how they are in the bedroom (or living room, or kitchen, or wherever). The greater the difference between the respectable, conventional personality displayed to the outside world (think of the prim librarian or besuited executive), and the wild, unrestrained nature of the sexual self, the more exciting the narrative is considered to be. For many readers—even those who have been brought up with no moral or ethical reservations about sex—excitement is all about losing control, losing inhibitions, losing one's dignity even, but in a safe, controlled, environment. What makes sex "dirty" to many people seems to be the fact that it involves a loss of control, a giving-in to some very basic instincts and urges. And in a culture that puts so much emphasis on self-control, self-discipline, and the dignity of the body—as testified by the modern cult of gym-hard muscles and the stigma attached to people who are obese, or who have otherwise "let themselves go"—this can seem very naughty indeed.

This kind of style is very different from the tone of most sex manuals and books like *The Joy of Sex*, which are always clinical, healthy, and clean, with realistic hand-drawn diagrams, "honest" discussions, arousal manipulation tips, foreplay do's and don'ts, discussions of the pros and cons of cunnilingus, and so on. This kind of rhetoric conveys the message that sex is a wonderful, healthy part of the way we are, and that our sexual self is simply an extension of our everyday personality—but it also highlights Western culture's continuing inability to separate sex talk from the language of medicine.

The rhetoric of the average porn magazine or website, on the other hand, is full of references to "nasty" girls, "naughty" nymphos, and women who like it "down and dirty." If sex is so wonderful, natural, and healthy—as most medical literature assures us—then why do so many people also seem to want it to be "dirty"? Sex-positive feminists have argued that one of the functions of pornography is to have it both ways—to allow readers to *play* at being "naughty" and "dirty" as part of their natural, healthy sex lives. I would point out, however, that most fantasies have their roots in "genuine" characterological drives and desires.

To put it another way, there is something about sex in Western culture that separates it from the rest of our everyday lives. We wear clothes, for example, not just to keep warm and protect ourselves, but to remind us that we are *not*, in fact, like the rest of the animals—that we are better, higher, more civilized, creatures with language and consciousness. In other words, we live with the conviction that we are not *really* at the mercy of our instincts and impulses. And so for many people, the most erotic kinds of narratives are those which depict sex as something that makes us "lose control," feel "beside ourselves," want to do things that are "filthy" and "obscene" because it asserts our animal nature, despite all our arrogant pretensions to civilization and dignity. As Jack Morin explains in his book *The Erotic Mind* (1996), shame in Western culture has come to be seen as an erotic lubricant.

Of course, the association between sex and shame is bound up with all kinds of other aspects of human culture, most notably religion, which for centuries has used the notion of shame to keep people separate and in the dark about their sexual desires and practices, and afraid of the social repercussions of openness. The "guilty" aspect of human sexuality is also bound up with the development of clothing and, interestingly enough, the history of architecture. In cultures and historical periods where families have lived in very close quarters, sex has been as much a part of everyday life as eating and sleeping. For the Victorian working classes, for example, sex was never as private as it was for the bourgeoisie, and therefore never considered as shameful or guilt inducing. And for cultures in which people regularly go unclothed, and for whom sex is a fairly public matter, the appeal of "naughty girls" and "nasty nymphos" would be completely undecipherable.

Distinctions of Gender

A significant element of much contemporary pornography is its tendency to graphically overdetermine the differences between men and women. Both softcore and hardcore porn generally involve an exaggerated focus on the difference between the two genders, which also results in a minimal interest in conflicts and contradictions as they are experienced within female identity, and this is one of the many ways in which pornography allows itself to be abstracted from the cause of women's oppression. The essence of most popular pornographic depictions resides not in any static representation of maleness or femaleness, but from a game of differences—not only physical differences, but (especially) differences in terms of conventions, attitudes, dress, emotions, gestures, feelings, implications, personality, and so on. The function and meaning of any erotic word, picture or image depends for its power on its association with other elements, to which it harks back, and refers forward. The stories and picture captions in pornographic magazines depend for their eroticism not only on static depictions of women, but on an interplay of the differences between women and men. This, and not simply the sexuality in the scenario depicted, is (supposed to be) the turn-on.

Such narrative stories invariably feature insistent references to the physical differences between women and men, to bodily parts, colloquial terms for sexual organs and so on, generally described in a style that relentlessly restates, through an endless variety of synonyms, the attributes of physical difference. Often, these differences are to do with dress. "Adult" magazines, far more than films and videos, often pay a surprising amount of attention to what one might have considered to be the minor matter of costume: women's clothes in particular are regularly described in extremely close detail, with particular focus on buttons, fasteners, lace, straps, and heels—an emphasis that might contain subliminal elements of bondage. One story in *Rustler* magazine, for instance, includes a character named Louise, who appears with "swept-up black hair, crisp white blouse, black pencil skirt, black seamed stockings and black patent shoes with heels neither too high nor too low." Underneath, she wears "dip-fronted briefs" with "a lacy panel hiding her womanhood" that she soon drops, "stepping out of them ever so delicately but keeping on her stockings and suspenders, held neatly in place with a black lace garter, fastened with a tiny red silk rose." And in another story in the same magazine, a "reader's wife" explains how she "put on a pair of white, textured pumps with small bows on the back. That was all, save for a pale silk G-string and white fishnets held up with a white-lace garter."

At other times, the differences between women and men have less to do with costume or even physical appearance than attitude, speech, mood, gesture, and situation. When the narrator of a "Reader's Letter" in *Rustler* describes his lover, for example, he informs us that "she had a refreshing, engaging naïvètè about her which I loved." The same issue contains a story about a rough stablehand who seduces a teenage horse-lover in a barn, and a story entitled "My True-Life Romance," which involves a teenage girl who, being sent down into the school store room to fetch some chalk, ends up having sex in a variety of positions with the school janitor. The eroticism of such stories arises less from the static depiction of women, or of sexual acts, than on a series of insistent themes and concepts based on the relentless restating, renaming and redetermining of physical, emotional, gesticular, attitudinal, psychological, and idiomatic differences between women and men.

There are a number of reasons to account for this tendency. Freud was perfectly clear in *Three Essays on the Theory of Sexuality* that to be anatomically "male" or "female" is no simple matter. Bisexuality and polymorphism are central to his theory, and, moreover, he realized there was no one-to-one correspondence between anatomical maleness and masculinity on one hand, and anatomical femaleness and femininity on the other. In "Three Essays," Freud explains how "Science . . . draws our attention to the fact that portions of the male sexual apparatus also appear in women's bodies, although in an atrophied state, and vice versa in the alternative case. It regards their concurrence as indicators of bisexuality, as though an individual is not a man or a woman but always both—merely a certain amount more one than the other" (38). In the same essay, Freud uses homosexuality to demonstrate that for the sexual drive there is no "natural," automatic object. He uses so-called sexual abnormalities to show that the sexual drive has no fixed aim. As Freud illustrates, since "normality" itself is a kind of ideal fiction and there is no qualitative (evaluative) distinction between "normality" and "abnormality," innate factors cannot account for the direction of the sexual drive.

It is highly possible that porn fiction stubbornly overemphasizes the differences between the genders in an attempt to compensate for an unconsciously acknowledged lack of any innate sexual difference. If Lacan is right, and the content of the psyche is structured *through* language and the entry into culture, then a feminist critic might well argue that these pornographic stories play with the readers' implicit cultural beliefs. Through this "game" of emphasizing and overdetermining a series of distinct and evident differences between the genders, pornography attempts to present an idealized and unproblematic world—a utopia, even—where biological gender, and therefore (apparently) sexuality, manifests itself in every look, every gesture, every implication.

Be this as it may, the work of Lacan cannot, in the end, resolve the feminist objection that this reworking of orthodox Freudianism is highly problematic and contentious. There are many feminist critics of various schools who accuse Lacan of merely shifting the cause of women's oppression from men *per se* to the structural organization of society, language, and exchange, and a close analysis of pornographic fictions does little to refute this claim.

Tales of the Expected and Unexpected

Most pornographic movies seem to be based on a rather unusual paradox. On the one hand, porn purports to deliver its pleasure by "showing all there is to see," by familiarizing and demystifying the female body. On the other hand, watching ninety minutes of nonstop penetrative sex is about as sexually arousing, for most people, as looking at slabs of meat hanging on hooks in a slaughterhouse. To arouse the viewer, therefore, and to keep their interest, sex in a porn film is usually broken down into a series of sequences, each involving different sexual activities, partners, positions, combinations, and so on, creating something along the lines of a "narrative," however vestigial. The challenge that lies before the discerning pornographer, therefore, is to "show all there is to see," while at the same time holding enough back to fuel the impetus of a narrative—a series of plausible transitions from sequence to sequence— that will continue to hold the interest of the audience.

Inevitably, perhaps, most porn on the video and DVD market today is bland and unimaginative, characterized by its dullness of mis-en-scène, single settings, flat lighting, and insipid direction. Any potential narrative developments are quickly reduced to escalating variations on sexual activity smothered in over-the-top, post-production-dubbed moaning that really does little more than to highlight the pitiful absurdity of human sexual relationships. Individuals are reduced to a series of apparently disembodied members and organs that appear to function independently of both character and personality because of their constant isolation in the frame. "Plot" in the conventional sense is reduced to clichéd combinations of partners, couplings, and sexual stereotypes. Narrative impetus is always limited—there has to be enough to legitimize and carry the sexual action, but not so much that it gets in the way of the main function of the film, which is, after all, to keep the viewer in a constant state of sexual arousal. Porn is ultimately about bodies, not minds.

Perhaps the best place to look for the most imaginative sexual scenarios are in the "classic" porn films of the 1970s, like Gerard Damiano's infamous *The Devil in Miss Jones* (1972), or Radley Metzger's *The Opening of Misty Beethoven* (1976). Both films manage to capture an atmosphere of sophisticated decadence through the use of erotic symbolism (snakes, sculpture, exotic fruit) and sex scenes that are both lusty and playfully ironic at the same time. They also both feature character-driven plots on a level no longer seen in adult film, and their stars—Constance Money and Georgina Spelvin—are older and more ordinary looking than most modern porn actresses, with natural breasts, unlaquered hair, and unshaven pubic areas.

The Devil in Miss Jones is a film wherein the sex scenes are prefaced by a thoughtful narrative build-up, emphasizing the protagonist's loneliness, inexperience, and sexual frustration. Consequently, the sex, when it occurs, is all the more appreciated, erotic, and satisfying. *The Opening of Misty Beethoven* is equally sophisticated, featuring a couple of lesbian sequences in which both parties are fully, even formally dressed—in business suits, stockings, silk blouses, and strings of pearls. Sequences like these seem far more creative than the random sex scenes in much contemporary porn, with its representative harsh lighting, silicon-heavy starlets, and obsession with anal sex.

These "classic" porn films, like "classical" Hollywood cinema in general, have a beginning, a middle, and an end—all of which are causally related—as well as a number of well-defined characters. In the typical contemporary porn movie, however, the "action" is often already running when the film opens, and we proceed directly to the climax, or the first in a series of climaxes, with "character" being replaced by a fragmented series of body parts and sexual organs. Nevertheless, this creative wasteland has been the breeding-ground for a small number of porn movies whose directors have proved that there is, indeed, a place in porn for imagination, wit, and even plot. Rather than being confined by the usual limitations of the genre, these directors—particularly Jane Waters, Domingo Lobo, Gregory Dark, Radley Metzger, and Rob Black—have utilized porn's apparent handicaps to make some provocative, entertaining, and memorable features.

One of the more interesting variants on the traditional porn formula is the movie that sets itself up as a pseudo-"documentary" or "behind-the-scenes exposé" into the steamy world of hard core. This is the kind of thing that Rob Black, the manager of porn video company Extreme Associates, seems to produce extremely well. For example, the 1998 feature *Asswoman in Wonderland*, directed by porn star Tiffany Mynx, begins with live footage from an Extreme Associates' employees chicken barbecue, where porn stars, producers, and dwarfs partake in natural, unscripted conversations around the picnic table. This "fly-on-the-wall" opening gradually segues into the scripted story itself, cued by the introduction of background music, as the impish Ms. Mynx starts to feel slightly squeamish after mixing prescription drugs with her beer. She leaves the party, and soon finds herself in a Lewis Carroll–inspired fantasy world, with an inevitable—yet nonetheless original—slant toward orgies, lesbianism, and anal sex.

Like all the best porn, *Asswoman in Wonderland* presents its sex scenes as a series of imaginative scenarios, rather than—as with so many contemporary films—simply going through the usual motions that lead up to the inevitable couplings, or presenting the same sexual peccadilloes again and again. While the sex scenes in *Asswoman* are fairly predictable, they are played out against an interesting background of hallucinatory colors, surreal dream sequences, cartoon-like characters, and mirror images (at one point, Ms. Mynx comes face-to-face with a vision of herself, strapped down on a chair in a lab, about to be examined by a pair of scientists). There's also an interesting S/M theme running throughout the film, a "little girl" motif—the protagonist wears an Alice-band, a long, Laura Ashley-style dress, opaque white stockings, and flat Mary-Jane shoes—and some intriguing oral symbolism featuring magic mushrooms and sacred elixirs, which places the film's action in a kind of magical realm.

The classic in "porno verité," however, is Jane Waters's film *The Pornographer*, also produced by Extreme Associates. Not a particularly erotic film, *The Pornographer* nonetheless presents fascinating glimpses of porn shoots in the "real world." We witness, among other things, the loose choreographing of sex sequences and camera angles, with mikes, booms, and cheap-looking hand-held video cameras clearly visible in most of the shots. An *al fresco* vignette is cut short because of the surfeit of annoying mosquitos, despite attempts to get rid of them with cigarette smoke blown upon the suffering human bodies by the ubiquitous Tiffany Mynx. We also see actors going for their thirty-day interval AIDS tests, "studs" taking Viagra before going on set, affectionate relationships between the foul-mouthed starlets, and a little bit of haggling over money.

Other ways to link sexual vignettes include the use of surrealism, irony, and tongue-in-cheek humor, as can be found in the work of Charles Pinion (a.k.a. Charley Crow), especially his movie *Archer's Last Day* (1999). Less overtly satirical, yet far more outrageous in tone is the work of Gregory Dark, director of the porn classic *New Wave Hookers* (1984). Dark's later films—*Snake Pit* (1996), *Living on the Edge* (1997), *Psychosexual* (1997), and *Psychosexual 2* (1999)—have little or no pretension to plot, yet are still interesting for their imaginative use of symbols.

The Erotic Olympics

A more consistently narrative-drive porn film is *The Erotic Olympics*, directed by Domingo Lobo and released for distribution in 1987. *The Erotic Olympics* stars porn stars Aunt Peg (Juliet Anderson), Bianca Perez, Herschel Steed, and Lindy Shaw, and is infused with a certain amount of self-consciousness toward the ultimately absurd nature of all pornography, and of human sexual relations in general. The film focuses on a pornographic film studio in California—run by a swinging couple, Sharon and Kenny Frick—which has started to encounter financial difficulties and cannot find enough new ideas or material to get back off the ground (a popular conceit in porn movies). In order to get the company out of the red, Sharon comes up with the idea of advertising a home video competition known as the First Annual Erotic Olympics, and inviting groups and couples to send in their home videos. There are four categories—Foreplay, Oral Sex, Intercourse, and Orgasm—and a prize of $50,000. According to their plan, Sharon and Kenny will be the judges of the competition, and award themselves the prize money for their own film, thus avoiding the necessity of coming up with $50,000, and winning themselves lots of original video material into the bargain.

The film's subplot involves a pornographic film and magazine agency, "Swingers Unlimited," run by Pamela Swanson (Aunt Peg) and her secretary, Trisha. When Sharon and Kenny place an ad for the Erotic Olympics in one of Ms. Swanson's magazines, she is both suspicious and intrigued. She decides to call the competition organizers and offer them $4,000 for a photo-spread of the winners of *The Erotic Olympics*. Kenny and Sharon arrive at the agency together with a cameraman—pretending to be the organizer of the competition—and his assistant Lisa, who presents Kenny and Sharon with the $4,000 check. However, during the orgy that ensues, the photographer, Danny, escapes with the check he was supposed to be splitting with Sharon and Kenny. Kenny chases after him, but it is too late. The following day, Sharon calls Ms. Swanson claiming that the check has bounced. Ms. Swanson calls Danny to find out what has happened, and Danny confesses that the whole competition is a fraud.

However, Ms. Swanson is still interested in *The Erotic Olympics* as a potential moneyspinner; she declares the contest still open, and gets her lawyer boyfriend, Gordon, to be an impartial judge. Gordon has a friend who owns a cable station, Bluetime Television, so the Erotic Olympics are broadcast late at night, and viewers are invited to call in and judge the videos. A phone number is broadcast after each video clip, and contestants are rated on a scale of 1–10. Gordon advises Ms. Swanson to make her own video and enter it into the competition, so she is taped during a sex session in the gym with the agency's "biggest hunk." The finalists of the Erotic Olympics are Kenny and Sharon Frick, Connie and Annie Lingus, The Foreskins, Hyman Schwartz and Hilda Reichbaum, and The Grand Rapids Swingers Club, but the competition is won by Pamela Swanson and friend, who gain 29 percent of the final vote. When Kenny and Sharon admit they are unable to pay her the $50,000 prize money, she agrees they can pay her off in product, by posing for a series of center-spreads in "Swingers Unlimited," which is what they are doing—on a pool table—as the movie ends.

Owing to the nature of its plot, *The Erotic Olympics* is a film full of orgy sequences. This tendency is not entirely representative of the genre, since most porn films generally feature couples, or threesomes, rather than full-blown orgies, presumably because the latter are rather difficult to stage, and even more difficult to film. Before moving on to look at a more typical example of the genre—the compilation film—I want to look at *The Erotic Olympics* in some detail, because this is a film which shares pornography's concerns with the merging human body, but does so in an especially lucid and formal manner, through an unusually coherent—if conventionalized—narrative. In *The Erotic Olympics*, orgy scenes are contained in the videos sent in by The Grand Rapids Swingers Club and The Foreskins—a punk band consisting of four skinheads who all dress in black rubber masks and beat one another up with chains. Two further orgies take place during the screening of the competition videos, both involving Ms. Swanson, her secretary, the photographer's assistant, another colleague from "Swingers Unlimited," and Kenny and Sharon Frick.

These orgy scenes are full of mass separation and disunion, with many scenes of fragmentation, where the body is "split" and divided in an extremely fetishized way, the camera separating breasts, genitals, buttocks, and faces from more conventional depictions of the whole person. In Lacanian terms, such depictions could be seen as an attack on the notion of the coherent self and a questioning of the notion that each of us has a clearly defined identity, self, or personality. If we take on board the Freudian concept of the unconscious, we must acknowledge that large parts of ourselves are subconscious and disintegrated. The orgy scenes in *The Erotic Olympics*, which split up bodies into a series of parts and organs, could be seen as manifesting what Lacan refers to as the violent deconstruction of the self, the inevitability of psychic fragmentation, and the division behind each individual's proclaimed subjective identity.

This can be substantiated by the fact that these orgy scenes very closely resemble Lacan's descriptions of the child at the mirror phase as an undifferentiated mass of uncoordinated limbs, suggesting no distinction between subject and object, and no clear, conscious sense of genderized self. In the *Ecrits*, Lacan explains how:

> The *mirror stage* is a drama . . . which manufactures for the subject, caught up in the lure of spatial identification, the succession of phantasies that extends from a fragmented body image to a form of its totality . . . This fragmented body . . . usually manifests itself in dreams . . . which encounter a certain level of aggressive disintegration in the individual. (4)

The main orgy sequences in *The Erotic Olympics* occur in the video sent into the competition by The Grand Rapids Swingers Club. In these scenes, the fragmentation of bodies becomes so confused that it is virtually impossible to work out which body parts belong to which character—and, occasionally, even which parts are male or female. These orgies comprise the main substance of the film, and—despite this film's superiority to most porn movies—details such as storyline, psychological interest, subtlety, and characterization are allowed to collapse completely. These and other elements become minor details that are seldom even considered.

Most of the characters, moreover, are fairly one-dimensional; no-one seems to have any hesitation about changing partners or coupling with strangers. We learn nothing about the history of Ms. Swanson's relationship with Gordon; the women are all bisexual and multiorgasmic; nobody seems to have any significant sexual inhibitions; we never learn the names of the "hunk" in the gym or the agency colleague. The basic plot of the film consists of highly contrived build-ups to the next graphic coupling. Ms. Swanson has a lesbian encounter on her office desk with her secretary; Sharon and Kenny make love in the polystyrene packaging from their new home video recorder; everybody has sex while watching the competition videos; and Ms. Swanson goes home to have sex with Gordon by the fireside.

These orgiastic scenes of division, dissolution, bisexual splitting and fragmentation are graphic physical descriptions of Lacan's rejection of the assumption that there is a gendered identity that is our real one, whatever our actual behavior. This assertion can be reinforced by Lacan's illustrations, in the *Ecrits*, that the most fundamental concepts in Freudian psychoanalysis are a return to psychic division, the splitting of the ego, and the endless (or "insistent") pressure of the unconscious against any individual's pretension to a smooth and coherent psychic and sexual identity. "For Lacan," writes Jacqueline Rose (1996), "psychoanalysis does not offer an account of a developing ego which is not *necessarily* coherent, but of an ego which is necessarily *not* coherent, that is, which is always and persistently divided against itself" (186).

A counterargument to this theory might be that bodily fragmentation should not necessarily be equated with the fragmentation of gender or identity. In these pornographic scenarios, however, the two are obviously quite closely related. Not only the bodily form, but also notions of *character* suffer a collapse. Porn stars as fictional characters either retain their "porn star" identity and appear in the movies as "John C. Holmes, the handy handyman" and so on, or else, as in *The Erotic Olympics*, their reality becomes subsumed by the fiction, and even in the film's credits, they *become* Aunt Peg, Viper, Savannah, or Johnny Wadd.

Loose Ends II

Since the special combination of graphic couplings and narrative cohesion in *The Erotic Olympics* is not especially typical of pornography, I now want to turn my attention to a more representative style of porn, the compilation film. *Loose Ends II* was directed by Bruce Seven and released as a sequel to an earlier film, *Loose Ends* (the dates of both films are unclear). The compilation film, unlike the sustained narrative, is comprised of a fusion of shorter clips from a selection of separate hardcore shorts, with little or no attempt at narrative cohesion. Such tapes feature nothing more imaginative than scene after scene of ejaculation with only the most minimal of narrative connection as they go through their own all-too-familiar formulaic paces: oral, anal, dildo, double penetration, money shot. Films like these seem to be set in some strange netherworld governed by the dregs of hallucinatory fantasy, where all men are hung like stallions and all women are tireless—a sort of hardcore Disneyworld wherein sex is utopian, unstoppable, without anguish, and without affection.

In *Loose Ends II*, opening selections from French and Italian movies feature a lesbian bedroom scene, a hospital sequence including the application of an enema, and an S/M featurette where a female victim is chained down by her ankles and breasts, and has hot wax dripped slowly over her breasts and genitals by a sinister group of masked men.

The main body of *Loose Ends II* consists of a long extract from a German porn film set in and around a white, castle-like building which functions as a health farm. The arrival of various guests—alone, in couples, and in groups—allows for a wide variety of couplings. One small group makes love in a swimming pool; two women and their masseuse enjoy a lesbian encounter in the bath, and other mixed groups couple in the shower and sauna. This is followed by an extended scenario featuring a single woman being ravished by a large group of healthy looking German men in the jacuzzi, and a scene involving a woman being tied down to a board and experimented with by a group of white-coated "scientists" using various electronic instruments.

The final section of *Loose Ends II*, unconnected to the previous sequences, consists of a lengthy series of ejaculation shots (minus their build-up) culled from a selection of European porn. This section features shots of disembodied male organs ejaculating on women, either singly or in groups, or—more frequently—on women's breasts, faces, legs, thighs, buttocks, stomachs, and hair. These shots are all fairly short, and—when they involve speech—include a variety of languages, changing rapidly from German, to English, to Swedish, to French, sometimes dubbed and sometimes not. Indeed, the quality of picture and soundtrack in *Loose Ends II* is abysmal, presumably due to constant amateur cutting, copying, and mixing for release to different countries, and to account for each country's censorship regulations. The dubbing, in particular, is exceptionally bad, so that characters—when they do speak—speak a dated idiomatic American English, and often at inappropriate moments.

The main goal of adult sexuality is often described as a return to a kind of oneness, or a merging with the other person. Sexual intercourse is often described as the temporary relinquishment of separating boundaries, or a situation in which the reciprocal interdependence—as experienced in genderless, pre-mirror stage early childhood—is recreated. Adult sexuality echoes aspects of mother–infant preverbal sexuality in a number of different ways, and presentations of mass sexuality and merger often stir up deeply resonant, early physical experiences recalled from before the mirror phase, before there was a definite sense of *self*— before gender, and before language. Sexuality often incorporates pre-Oedipal pleasures of merging and fusion, rather than Oedipal issues of separation and individuation.

It has been observed that the reexperiencing of infantile states in sexual relationships is often depicted in psychoanalysis as if it were a relatively safe and satisfying experience. In fact, however, this merging can only ever be partial and temporary (whereas the infantile state, in contrast, is total and timeless), since we are, in the end, adults, and retain some awareness of this, and our capacity to return to the adult state should we desire to do so. Also, the reexperiencing of infantile states in adult sexual relationships is often painful, and full of conflict.

However, in *Loose Ends II*—partly because of its very poor quality and the haphazard way it is pieced together—this merging is total and continuous, rarely painful, and never conflicting. The scenes in the swimming pool, bathroom, shower, sauna, and jacuzzi present scenes of bisexual merger and fusion, unbroken by plot, dialogue, or narrative intervals, except to incorporate the changing of partners, or the introduction of new sexual variations. This unbroken pornographic otherworld suggests a return to the mirror phase, characterized by the inability to make any distinction between self and others, and by the absence of gender difference. These kinds of primal fictions can be read, by feminists and others, as artifacts which disintegrate notions of ego, since they resemble a primal, genderless cultural unconscious that preexists the splitting of the subject.

We need to understand the ways in which the word "utopian" can be applied to the compilation film, because in its continuous sequences of orgies and ejaculations, we encounter a profoundly escapist and bisexual genre that distracts audiences from the deeper social or political causes of the disturbed relations between the sexes. The compilation film presents a place where people are transformed into objects, which finally all coalesce into one object, or one self. This place is similar to Lacan's Imaginary Order described in the *Ecrits*—also a world of plenitude, of merger without cessation, without lacks or exclusions, without the inequities of sexual difference. Porn films like this represent sex without beginning or end, and these images of the merger and fusion of the body suggest that what such films are depicting is, if not the symbolic realization (for the voyeur) of the incestuous fantasy, then a homecoming to the Imaginary Order.

The Beast

I now want to turn my attention to another kind of film—a more "upmarket" movie originally released on the arthouse circuit in the United States, where it still remains uncertified, though it is now also available in VHS and DVD versions. *The Beast* (*La Bête*) was made in 1983 by Czech director Walerian Borowczyk, and is perhaps best defined as an erotic thriller, because—unlike the less thoughtful porn films discussed in this chapter—it actually has a fairly complex storyline (see figure 5.1).

The film opens with the protagonist, Lucy Broadhurst, being driven to a French château in the middle of a dark forest where she is to meet and marry her cousin Mathurin de l'Espérance, to whom ancient family connections have betrothed her. When Lucy and her mother arrive at the castle, however, things are not quite as they expected. Mathurin is brusque and peevish, interested only in watching his horses copulate in the courtyard. Mathurin's father, the Marquis de l'Espérance, seems desperate to contact his cousin the Archbishop, who alone has the power to bless the marriage, thereby dispelling an ancient family curse.

One of the film's many subplots involves Mathurin's hippy sister, who takes every opportunity she can find to engage in (constantly inter-rupted) sex with Ifany, the family's black butler—even to the extent of hiding two children she is supposed to be babysitting in Ifany's bedroom closet for the sake of privacy. Each time they start having sex, Ifany is called downstairs, and his frustrated lover ends up masturbating on the bedpost.

Figure 5.1 *The Beast* (Walerian Borowczyk, 1983)

After taking a number of graphic photos of Mathurin's copulating horses with her new camera, Lucy discovers a strange old book in her bedroom at the château. The book contains illustrations of men and women coupling with beasts, and these pictures lead Lucy to masturbate. Later, Mathurin's grandfather shows her another ancient journal that once belonged to a family ancestor, Lady Romelda. This journal details the place in the castle grounds where, according to Romelda, "I met him and overcame him," and includes marginal sketches of a strange, ape-like beast with an enormous phallus.

That afternoon, Mathurin sends Ifany to present Lucy with a single red rose on a gold platter. Lucy, highly curious about this mysterious family and excited about her forthcoming wedding, begins to masturbate with the rose, crushing it petal by petal into her vagina while she falls into a daydream. In her dream, Lucy becomes the Lady Romelda, dressed as a shepherdess, searching the castle grounds for a lost lamb. Upon discovering the lamb's mangled corpse, she gets involved in a violent chase with a huge beast—a bizarre-looking creature, half-wolf, half-ape, with a gigantic penis. Lucy/Romelda manages to escape up a tree, dropping one of her shoes in the process, which the beast finds and masturbates into. She is unable to escape for long, however, and the beast eventually captures her and engages her in a variety of sexual acts, which she quickly comes to enjoy. Here, the narrative flashes back and forth between Lucy/Romelda being ravished by the beast in the forest, and Lucy daydreaming in her bedroom, masturbating with the rose sent to her by Mathurin.

In Lucy's daydream, the beast constantly pumps out a stream of milky semen from his enormous penis; the seduction scene does not end until he topples over and dies "of ecstasy." Lucy/Romelda runs away, ashamed at what she's done. Meanwhile, back in the castle, awaking from her daydream, Lucy creeps into Mathurin's bedroom, only to find his body lying dead on the floor. When the Archbishop arrives the following morning to conduct the wedding, he is called upon instead to consecrate Mathurin's corpse. When the body is unveiled, we see that Mathurin was possessed of a small but substantial animal's tail that twitches when sprinkled with holy water. It turns out that Mathurin was the offspring of the Lady Romelda's coupling with the beast—hence his fondness for horses, his sister's preference for the black butler, and so on. The Archbishop speaks the closing words of the film—a quotation from Leviticus: "if a woman approaches any beast and lies with it, you shall kill the woman and the beast; they shall be put to death, their blood is upon them."

The Beast is full of Freudian thematic clusters. Central to the film is the concept of parents and children, brothers and sisters, mothers and daughters, the extended family and its "hidden secret"—something of a sexual nature—mingled with the theme of incest (Lucy and Mathurin are cousins) aired not with unblinking directness as a confronted taboo, but closely explored as an erotic fantasy. The image of Mathurin's sister hiding her children in a bedroom closet while she has sex is an obvious representation of the primal scene, discussed by Freud in *Three Essays on the Theory of Sexuality*.

More significantly, perhaps, is the relationship presented in the film between present and past. The whole plot is steeped in references to a former plot, to something ineradicable that happened in the past, whose effects are felt every day in the present. Every member of the family is influenced in their character and sexuality by a traumatic event that happened in the past. In *The Beast*, the past pervades the present—its influences are everywhere, most notably in the form of the Lady Romelda's drawings and journals. One important aspect of the film is its scrutinizing of the traumatic starting point of sexual awareness, and the sexual deviations that have a propensity to recur throughout generations of a family. The film deepens its scope by constantly delving into the family's history to come up with earlier instances of strange sexual aberrations.

What is most significant about *The Beast*, however, is that it is a film full of fetishes. Pictures and images become a fetish for Lucy. She is fascinated by the portrait of Romelda hanging in the drawing room; she gazes at the pictures in Romelda's journal; she masturbates over the pictures of copulating horses. Lucy, in fact, is something of a voyeur, and her relationship with pictures at least gives the illusion of being more concrete and direct than her relationship with the words in the colorless Bible her mother gives her to read. Mathurin, in turn, is obsessed with the sexuality of his horses; his sister is obsessed with the African butler; she masturbates using the bedpost; Lucy masturbates with a rose; the beast masturbates with Romelda's shoe. In fact, there is no "ordinary" sex in this film.

From a Lacanian perspective, *The Beast* shows how desire has a remarkably substitutive nature; anything and everything in Borowczyk's film comes to stand in for the object of desire. Lacan explains that as we enter into the Symbolic Order, all objects are lost, and the breast, or mother, must be given up by the child. Lacan also explains that the whole of infantile and adult sexuality—including genital sexuality, which is usually considered the "normal" route for sexual instincts—is perverted or abstracted from its original object. Consequently, all desire is always imbued with the qualities of substitution and displacement. In *The Beast*, this desire is directed toward animals, objects, pictures, flowers, items of clothing, dreams, even the female body itself. All function as fetish substitutions for something that can never be recovered. According to Lacan, we need to recognize that gender, sexual fantasy, and sexual desire derive fundamentally from mystifications and infantile misrecognitions of what Kaja Silverman (1988) refers to as "lost objects and mistaken subjects" (36). From a Lacanian perspective, Borowczyk's film suggests that all adult and infantile sexual desire is a substitution of one kind or another.

Fetish Substitutions

In fact, all types of sexual desire manifested in pornography are substitutions, since the original object of desire has been lost, and can never be reclaimed. The difficulty at the heart of being human to which psychoanalysis and its objects of inquiry—sexuality and the unconscious—bear witness, is the Lacanian paradigm that the subject is split, and the object is lost. To pass through the mirror phase is to enter society and the Symbolic Order of language, which symbolizes what has been lost when the child emerges from the mirror phase. What has been lost is the mother's body, the child's relationship to it, and that lack of distinction between self and others characteristic of early childhood, and of the mother's womb—a state figured in the mergers and fusions of various pornotopias.

The issue of a pro-pornography argument within feminist readings of Lacan lays open a number of other interesting thoughts about the nature of pornography. The substance and power of pornography seems to me to lie not, as many feminists have claimed, in its intrinsic connections with violence and rape, nor in its "objectification" of women, nor in any particularly new or particularly bizarre sexual deviances. I have come to believe, as a woman, that porn is chiefly remarkable in the way it elicits the emotions of a primal state, unconsciously testifying to a new kind of understanding of the mirror phase, of difference, and of the division between Imaginary and Symbolic.

Yet any feminist reading of Lacan must remain highly aware of the dangers and limitations of Lacanian theory, many of which I have already touched upon. Other feminist critics have convincingly argued that Lacanian and post-Lacanian explanations of the construction of a gendered subjectivity have been important in cultural analysis only for a narrowly defined intellectual audience, for whom advocacy of the need for change in cultural practices—other than aesthetics—lies outside their terrain. This is an especially weighty argument in the case of porn, a genre whose audience tends to be almost wholly male and mainly nonacademic. It is important to be aware of the irony involved in applying a feminist intellectual practice to a popular male genre. Cora Kaplan (1988) points out that semiotic and psychoanalytic perspectives have yet to be integrated with social, economic, and political analysis. She argues that critics tend to privilege one element or the other, even when they acknowledge the importance of both, and the need to relate them.

Yet surely one of the essential properties of feminist theory is its capacity to allow female readers to appropriate nonfeminist texts, however ironic such readings may initially seem to be. "Women," argues Andrea Dworkin in her lurid book on pornography (1981), "will finally be free when pornography no longer exists" (64). My own exploration of the nature of pornography has led me to believe, on the contrary, that a feminist appropriation of Lacan allows women to understand that pornography itself represents a new kind of freedom. This is a freedom not only to depict gender in radical and symbolic ways, but also—and more importantly—to represent complex psychological conditions with an uncommon power and lucidity.

CHAPTER 6

DARK HOMECOMINGS: LACAN AND HORROR FICTIONS

In England, in 1983, the *Daily Mail* newspaper ran a vociferous campaign against what it identified as a sudden new plague—a heavy increase in the manufacture and popularity of explicit uncensored horror videos, or "video nasties," which apparently occurred alongside the new market for home VCR players. These new "video nasties," according to the *Daily Mail*, "are not spine-chillers in the tradition of Conan Doyle or Edgar Allan Poe. They are soul-spoilers that deaden decency and encourage depravity." The newspaper made the claim that these "video nasties," quite unlike other horror films available for the home VCR market, were "utterly foul, and unbelievably evil."

These kinds of media "panics" about horror movies seem to occur on a regular basis. In 1978, in his book *Caligari's Children*, S. S. Prawer complained that "I feel myself borne along by yet another wave of terror films, a wave whose crest is formed by what are frequently called 'meat' or 'road accident' movies—films like *The Texas Chainsaw Massacre*, which provide shock through the maximum exhibition of flesh in the process of being mangled and blood in the process of being spilt" (15).

Moral panics about a new wave of particularly violent horror, whether in film or fiction, are nothing new. Nor is this particular controversy limited solely to those "low" horror movies that have proliferated in the last thirty years. Indeed, for the publishers of horror comic books, at least in England, this particular moral panic has been going on ever since the Children and Young Persons (Harmful Publications) Act of 1955, during which the Comics Campaign Council claimed that large numbers of ordinary people, often quite independently of one another, noticed their children reading American-style comics. According to Martin Barker in his book on this subject, *A Haunt of Fears* (1984), "they were horrified by their contents, and immediately acted to get something done about them" (9).

It would be wrong to conclude that these comics were directed solely toward children, because many issues had a wide readership among adults as well. Since 1950, the popularity in Britain of issues like *Crypt of Terror* (rereleased by Amicus in 1972 as *Tales from the Crypt*) has suggested the existence of a thriving market for adult strips that are far removed from the children's material on shop stands. *Crypt of Terror* was always a magazine that adults could feel comfortable with due to its plethora of intertextual references to more "highbrow" or adult fiction, such as the works of Edgar Allan Poe and Ray Bradbury.

In non-comic format, horror fiction has long been popularized by the commercial successes of authors like Stephen King, James Herbert, Clive Barker, and Neil Gaiman, although Barker and Gaiman have also used the comic book format in works like *Night Visions* (1986) and *Sandman* (1989). Although their form and manifestation may alter and develop from tense mood-piece to apocalyptic "meat movie," explicit horror fictions, like explicit porn films, are clearly nothing new. Looking at earlier as well as more recent manifestations of the horror genre, in this chapter I examine first the various branches of horror criticism, paying particular attention to the psychoanalytic field. Second, I question the major Freudian tenets on which most recent psychoanalytic criticism of horror fictions is based; and third, I attempt to explain how Lacanian psychoanalysis provides a more relevant and satisfactory methodology for explaining how the recurrent themes and motifs of many horror stories are, as with pornography, themselves in liaison with the workings of unconscious discourse.

Horror and Critical Theory

Outside of psychoanalysis, horror criticism has generally situated the text in its cultural or historical context, presenting a dystopian, generally ideological vision of the consumer gradually becoming reconciled to the prevailing cultural or social policy, or the dominant ideology. For example, in *A Haunt of Fears* his sociopolitical study of the British campaign against American-style comic books of the 1950s and 1960s, critic Martin Barker notes that it became apparent during his investigations just how much the Comics Campaign Council had depended on the organized intervention of the British Communist Party, who wanted to stop American influences on young children. Zombie films are often explained in similarly dystopian terms suggesting ideological undertones—Vietnamese or Korean hordes coming after "us" in human waves, or, better yet, ghouls as the "silent majority."

James Twitchell, in his book *Dreadful Pleasures* (1985), analyzes zombie films by referring to their ethnocentric perspectives. He debates whether the myth of zombies developed before or after the slaves left Africa for the United States, analyzing how closely Hollywood's voodoo tradition comes to the original traditions of Haiti and the Caribbean. In other words, he questions whether Hollywood's version of the zombie myth may or may not be a cultural condensation of life under white rule from a black point of view (64). Films like *Invasion of the Body Snatchers* (1956) are generally analyzed as clever fictionalizations of the horrors of paranoia and McCarthyistic thought. Many critics have studied *King Kong* (1933) in terms in the way in which the ape's predicament parallels that of the African American—because Kong himself is black, and because he is wrenched from his African homeland by white people who want to exploit him.

Christian Metz, in his book *Language and Cinema* (1974), regarded the audience or consumer as becoming "reconciled" to a "dominant ideology" when he described the (implicitly "culturally deprived") mass audience in terms of "disavowal"—the easy suspension of disbelief, the eagerness to feign ignorance of how the fiction is going to end (63). Most contemporary criticism on horror fictions is less aesthetic than ideological, and seems to suggest that such fictions are worth studying because they are so popular, and not because they are interesting, fruitful, or aesthetically valuable in and of themselves.

The very volume of this ideological criticism of horror fictions suggests that, if nothing else, this type of horror is an established genre, a fixed cultural pattern, and so, by its nature, by its very familiarity, it inclines toward reassurance. A culturally defined genre invites culturally defined criticism, and this very familiarity leads to the citing of the text within a recognized social, cultural, and political environment. Of course this is vital. Nevertheless, such criticism, while emphasizing the role of the consumer in terms of social policy, tends to rely on the "moral neutrality" of the social sciences, which, to a large extent, does not allow for an aesthetic appreciation of the text.

Other critics have elected to analyze horror in relation to Tsvetan Todorov's theories of the fantastic and the sublime (1981). For example, James Donald, in the introduction to his book *Fantasy and the Cinema* (1989) analyzes Dreyer's *Vampyr* in terms of the history and ideology of the fantastic, and considers "the tackier" forms of popular culture with reference to Toderov's theories of fantasy, and Kant's version of the modern sublime. Michal O'Pray (1989) studies Jan Svankmajer's films in terms of the use of the grotesque and the uncanny, the use of marionettes, puppets, and other such effigies, and the distinction between fantasy and phantasy. Similarly, Raymond Bellour (1988) analyzes Hitchcock in terms of Barthes's theory (1975) of the text being "starred" or "constellated" with a number of different "lexes" (see chapter 3). In his analysis of Hitchcock's *Psycho* (1960), for example, Bellour suggests that Marion, Norman, and Norman's mother are linked together as associations across a complex and interrelated set of cinematic and narrative codes, which center on the notions stuffed/mummified/dead, threat/penis/knife, and looking/object of look/voyeurism.

There is also, of course, a substantial branch of feminist film criticism, led by Laura Mulvey's seminal essay, "Visual Pleasure and Narrative Cinema" (1988). Feminist film critics tend to interpret film in terms of the (male) scopophilic gaze. Mulvey discovers where and how the fascination of film is reinforced by preexisting patterns of fascination already at work within the individual subject and the social formations that have molded him (Mulvey intentionally uses the male third-person singular to stand in for the spectator because she is interested in the relationship between the image of the woman on screen, and the "masculinization" of spectator position, regardless of actual gender). Mulvey concludes that the scopophilic instinct (the pleasure of looking at another person as an erotic object) and, in contradistinction, the ego–libido (the forming identification processes) act as formations and mechanisms which cinema has played on (and this is of particular importance for the analysis of pornographic films). Following Mulvey, Constance Penley (1988) discusses the strong current in feminist criticism that rejects contemporary theoretical approaches like those of Freud and Lacan on the grounds of their implicitly masculine bias, consequently adapting alternative theories, or even bypassing theory altogether, by way of a direct appeal to experience, or to a specifically feminine understanding of the world. Other feminist film critics, including Kaja Silverman (1988), Janet Bergstrom (1988), Joan Copjec (1995), and Mary Ann Doane (1988), all present highly original discussions of Mulvey's theoretical assumption that classical film narrative, if not the entire cinematic apparatus, is geared toward male fascination, and the structures of male voyeuristic pleasure.

However helpful much of this feminist film criticism may be in analyzing the masculine bias of cinevisual conventions, its involvement with ideological issues tends to subsume the aesthetics of the source material. In other words, its emphasis on a mostly critical analysis of mostly male cinematic perspectives does not allow for any purely aesthetic appreciation of the merits of the films themselves. Although it is of particular use in the theoretical analysis of pornography (see chapter 5), little of this body of feminist criticism is directed exclusively toward the horror genre in particular. Moreover, those feminist critics whose works *do* concentrate on horror, such as Barbara Creed (1993), Joan Hawkins (2000), Vera Dika (1990), and Vivian Sobchack (1997), tend to focus on the most acceptable branches of the genre, rather than the more violent undercurrent of cinematic horror, which is the kind of film I intend to focus on most extensively in this chapter.

In fact, most criticism of the horror genre concentrates on the "epics," and either passes over more "lowbrow" movies in silence (as is the case in Noel Carroll's *The Philosophy of Horror* [1990]), or provides a simple, narrative account of the genre (as is the case in William Schoell's *Stay Out of the Shower* [1985]), or else bemoans it as a degenerate aberration (as is the case in David Hogan's *Dark Romance* [1986]). This critical refusal to come to terms with the "low" horror genre, like the critical refusal to come to terms with much of popular culture, seems rather imprudent and condescending, especially since those critics who *do* refer to this genre, including Robin Wood (1978), Carol J. Clover (1993), and Tania Modleski (1984), all generally acknowledge that the "low" horror film is quite progressive in its own perverse way.

Horror and Psychoanalysis

The majority of criticism—feminist and otherwise—written on the subject of horror fiction has been, in one way or another, psychoanalytic, partly because of the suitability of this kind of fetish-and-phobia material for psychoanalysis. The abundance of dream and nightmare material within most horror (and, incidentally, pornographic) movies amply testi-fies to the fertility of this kind of fiction for the psychoanalytic critic, whether Freudian or not. Elements of the horror text particularly ripe for psychoanalytic investigation include its shock tactics, its violent and often free-associated imagery, and the celebration of the supernatural and unreal. These are qualities which highlight the association between horror and surrealism, an association that can be traced back to Jean Epstein's film of *The Fall of the House of Usher*, where the director's assistant was Luis Bunûel, whose collaboration with Dali on *Un Chien Andalou* that same year (1928) fused surrealism with violent elements which suggest the Grand Guignol and later horror films. S. S. Prawer claims that the surre-alists professed great admiration for horror films, proclaiming approba-tion of "their involuntary poetry, their unexpected visual juxtapositions (*pouvoir de dépaysement*), their dream-quality, their celebration of *amour fou* and everything that is *délirant* and *convulsif*" (101).

These qualities are certainly evident in such horror films as David Cronenberg's *Videodrome* (1983), where the horror is video itself. In this film, a video "virus," devised by a McLuhanesque deluded scientist (Dr. Brian O'Blivion of the Cathode Ray Mission) emits infectious hallucinogenic rays that result in vivid, preprogrammed hallucinations (a television screen becomes a huge pair of lips, a video cassette is forced into a vaginal slot in the protagonist's stomach). Finally, the protagonist himself becomes no more than a videocassette, infected to rerun someone else's program of psychological hallucinations. Here, by suggesting a powerful awareness of the genre, by foregrounding its own signifying practice and by avoiding the temptation to regard itself as *ipso facto* realistic, the film begins consciously to betray its *own* version of the real as a relative one, which can deform and transform experience, so the "real" is exposed as just another ontological category.

As *Videodrome* suggests, the horror film has made much use of the nightmares described by the users of hallucinogenic drugs. It was, in fact, the fascination with narcotics (and particularly hallucinogens) in the 1960s that provided much of the imagery employed at that time by emerging horror films and comic book artists. A popular 1970s horror classic, *Blue Sunshine* (1976), plays on this theme, when a series of middle-aged, bourgeois ex-hippies suddenly become affected by the peculiar strain of LSD they took ten years earlier in 1966, when they were still flower children, and not the living dead.

It is Lacan's reworking of Freudian psychoanalysis that seems to provide the most fertile ground for an aesthetic study of horror fictions. In order to reach Lacan, however, we must begin with Freud, since most psychological dialectics have their roots in Freud's theories of the unconscious, and even Lacan declared himself to be a Freudian. Many critics of horror and porn have tried to interpret the fascination of their subject matter in relation to more traditional Freudian analysis of the body, and sexuality. For example, in his essay "Fetishism and the Horror Film," (1989) Roger Dadoun analyzes traditional horror movies in terms of transference fetishism, the castration of the mother, and male castration anxieties (represented by the stake, the crucifix, and so on).

Carol J. Clover, in her book *Men, Women and Chainsaws* (1993), suggests that the killer of the "slasher" movie is not just an eruption of the normally repressed sexual energy of the civilized male, but also of the power and potency of non-phallic sexuality. Her ultimate argument is that the "Final Girls" (last remaining survivors) of "slasher" films are actually men, or at least representations of men, beating (and therefore loving) other men. This homosexual fantasy, according to Clover, is displaced, in order to make it more acceptable to the (mainly male) audience of such films, but it suggested by the "male" names of the female victims (Stretch, Stevie, Marti, Will, Terry, Laurie, and Ripley). Significantly, however, Clover overlooks many notable "Final Girls" whose names are rather more feminine, with certain particularly feminine names proving especially popular, including Sally (*Texas Chainsaw Massacre* [1974]), Nancy (the *Nightmare on Elm Street* series [1984 onward], *Dressed to Kill* [1976]), and Alice (the *Friday the 13th* series [1980–1985], and *Nightmare on Elm Street* parts 4–5).

In her essay "Time Travel, Primal Scene and the Critical Dystopia," Constance Penley (1989) analyzes horror in terms of sexual difference, and in "Horror and the Monstrous-Feminine: An Imaginary Abjection," Barbara Creed uses Julia Kristeva's vital work *The Powers of Horror* (1982) to discuss horror as castratory, as a displacement of fear of the female genitalia. She also analyzes frightening phenomena (bodily organs, bodily wastes, and so on) as "breaking the borders," and therefore violating taboos. Working to a traditional Freudian schema, Creed (1989), like Penley, regards science fiction as a reworking of the primal scene in relation to different forms of copulation and procreation. Other psychoanalytic scholars have produced equally interesting work on the horror film. Jacqueline Rose, for example, in her book *States of Fantasy* (1996) looks at Hitchcock's *The Birds* (1963) as a feminist critique of psychoanalytic film theory examining the presumed sexual dysymmetry in the classical film's "point of view" system. Raymond Bellour, in his essay "Psychosis, Neurosis, Perversion" (1988), uses *Psycho* (1960) to reply to Rose's critique, presenting his case in even stronger terms.

Classic Freudian Readings of Horror

Most critics writing on the horror film use Freudian theories of repression, whether of the castration complex (Dadoun), sexual energy (Clover), or primal scene (Creed), which pick up on Freud's version of the latency myth, where unexpressed emotions are kept "inside" us, until they are allowed to come "out," sometimes of their own accord. According to this theory, horror appeals to what is often described as a basic human need to articulate all those violent desires, terrors, and urges normally believed to be repressed in the unconscious. These emotions are sometimes described as the remnants of man's primal nature, the "beast within," or perhaps the anger, frustration, and desire stifled and repressed by civilization—a theory often used to explain the popularity of both pornography (see chapter 5) and the behavior of sports fans (see chapter 2). "The fantastic terror film," writes S. S. Prawer, "responds to a need one can observe in any fairground: the need to be safely frightened, the need to test and objectify and come to grips with one's fears in a setting of ultimate security" (48). Incidentally, this examination of the "repressed emotions" of the psyche in carefully controlled test-conditions is nothing new; Lovelace is already doing this in Richardson's *Clarissa* (1748) when he places the heroine in a brothel.

As Commander Adams informs Dr. Morbius in *The Forbidden Planet* (1956) "we are all part monsters in our subconscious. That's why we have laws and religion." On the Forbidden Planet, a sci-fi version of Prospero's enchanted island in *The Tempest*, sexual mores go seriously astray, and anger, desire, and frustration need to be carefully controlled. The horror text is often described as a failsafe vehicle for the articulation of these normally "dangerous" and therefore "repressed" unconscious desires, needs, and urges. In his work on literature and the unconscious, which follows the pathways of U.S. ego-psychology, Norman Holland (1990) expands on this rather dubious theory of art as carefully controlled catharsis (rather than, e.g., as symptom), and the last section of Wolfgang Iser's book *Prospecting* (1993) provides a different but related perspective of art as refreshing the norm by admitting aberrant material. Ideas about the sublime, such as Todorov's, might also be substantially relevant here.

The discovery of the repetition-compulsion, which was directed mainly toward frightening and traumatic material, led Freud to seek an explanation of such manifestations "beyond" the pleasure principle, because they are unpleasant. Erotic desire itself for Freud brings a tension that is not *itself* pleasurable, as Peter Brooks expounds in his book *Reading for the Plot* (1984). Investigation of the repetition-compulsion incited Freud to revise his earlier theories about instinct, and to posit these spontaneous manifestations of latent traumas as "death instincts," as opposed to "life instincts," for he could not deny the intensity—which he called "daemonic"—in such manifestations, which was closer to hate than to seeking after libidinal satisfaction.

Most of the popular explanations for the function and appeal of horror involve the way it is believed to articulate these "repressed emotions." Horror fictions are assumed to enact a cathartic purification of the mind from the "inner" unconscious desires, urges, energies, fears (of castration), memories (of the primal scene), needs (for release and violence), and so on. Writing horror stories, instead of going to a psychoanalyst's couch, insists British horror writer James Herbert in his book *Dark Places* (1999), enables him to get rid of all his phobias. "I'm getting all these nasty ideas out on to paper," he writes, suggesting that most people keep *their* "nasty ideas" somewhere inside their heads (31). Similarly, Stephen King, in his book *Danse Macabre*, claims that at the core of his writing is the conviction that we all contain a "potential lyncher" within us, and that there are "anti-civilization emotions," or "hungry alligators" that are "swimming around in that subterranean river beneath our civilized forebrains" that "need to be fed or let loose every now and then, and allowed to scream and roll around on the grass" if mental and social equilibrium is to be maintained from the satisfaction and release that follows the discharge of tension from a dammed-up need (19).

The notion of latency find perhaps its most articulate expression in Stanley Kubrick's *The Shining* (1977), set in an out-of-season ski hotel isolated by miles of snow-covered mountains. Both Stephen King's original novel and Kubrick's film are full of crafty horror and tightly enmeshed structural patterns, but the primary strength of both the film and the book are the beautifully organized tensions within the relationships of the central characters—the alcoholic Jack Torrance, his wife Wendy, their young son Danny, and a sympathetic outsider, Halloran. Jack's gradual transformation from quiet, civilized writer into violent, murderous psychopath is attributed to his "possession" by the spirit of the previous caretaker, who was driven "out of his mind" by the isolation, gave way to his repressed "inner rage" and butchered his wife and child. Simultaneously, Torrance's preternaturally gifted son descends into madness and schizophrenia when he begins to visualize his "inner fears," and, for him, the hotel is transformed from a wonderland into "a land full of sick wonders" reached through mirrors and "a round black hole" that leads "deep down inside yourself to a place where nothing comes through" (20). Little Danny Torrance has flashes of precognition and the power to "see" into the "inner side." But his power works in both ways: the "inner side" can see—and act—through Danny into the "here." In the end, the hotel becomes a battleground where Torrance fights a losing war against his "latent" murderous drives.

Despite its palatability as a comprehensive theory explaining our "less civilized" desires and urges, the idea of latency leaves much to be contested. There is something rather questionable, for example, about the common figurative spatialization of emotions that we fail to get "out" remaining somewhere "inside" us, waiting for such a time as they can come "out," possible of their own accord. The theory also suggests that "vicarious experience" of aggression and violence provides a relatively harmless release for "pent-up" aggressive instincts, and that it can therefore be of value in the socializing process. A similar argument is regularly put forward in favor of pro-pornography legislation (see chapter 5). Although popular and influential (especially among fans of horror and porn), this explanation appears to rest on the tenuous assumption that there exists some kind of exact, almost direct, ritualistic link between what is depicted in mass media images, and a set of allegedly subconscious instincts, emotions, and automatic nervous reactions that are claimed to exist in the mind of the consumer who decodes such images.

And even if such a magical connection exists, why should these "innate" feelings, when they do come out, be far fiercer and more dangerous than "conscious" urges—the type of emotion that has been in contact with "outside" reality and rational control? In his book *Terrors of Uncertainty* (1989), a sociological account of the popularity of horror fictions, critic Joseph Grixti remarks that as a result of the research on child-training practices in the development of aggression, the frustration–aggression hypothesis has been dismissed as a "fragile" explanation which is "less often advanced in serious studies of aggression than it is in popular or ideological writings" (21).

In many horror fictions, the repressed emotions we keep "inside" the unconscious form a personality of their own, which develops into our "alter ego," the "dark side" of our personality, our doppelganger. This simplification of Freud's writings on repression provides the basis for many readings of horror fictions (as well as pornography), including Roger Dadoun's notion of transference fetishism, and Carol J. Clover's concept of displacement. This idea that a positive/negative paradigm underlies the ego/id division finds its apotheosis in the legend of the werewolf, and in stories like *Dr. Jekyll and Mr. Hyde*, and generally presents one id-driven persona performing acts of violent carnal aggression, which, it is suggested, the host—and, by implication, we too—might secretly desire.

As a theme for story matter, this fiction of the Savant versus the Monster provides common stock for a wide range of texts. Steven Spielberg's *Jaws* (1975), for example, charts "civilization" as only a few steps away from savagery. The modern beach resort of Amity may indeed be a bustling vacation paradise (civilized ego), but just across the beach lies the paleolithic (uncivilized id). A number of other films are, often quite intentionally, less subtle.

For example, Ken Russell's *Altered States* (1980) involves a bright young intellectual who gets over-involved in research on yage and peyote, and enjoys experimenting with immersion in an isolation tank. After months spent hallucinating with South American Indians, the outwardly intelligent, sophisticated protagonist discovers that a dose of secret Indian potion coupled with lengthy spells in the isolation tank leads to the sporadic appearance of the "primitive, bestial" side of human nature, which increasingly continues to show itself even outside the tank, until it overtakes the protagonist completely, and he is transformed into a huge, murderous simian prowling the streets of New York. According to the popular version of Freud, this doppelganger motif is really the projection and diffusion of infantile desires that slip past the superego censors so the "double" can act independently of the central self.

As a common storyline, this notion is clearly successful, though there is much in it to be contested. Again, there is no particular reason *why* there should be any direct, magical link between things that happen to us, and our own unconscious instincts and autonomous nervous reactions, nor why the aggression of the secret "alter ego" (not a Freudian concept anyway) should be any more untamed and destructive than the type of anger and desire that has been in contact with "outside" reality and rational control. The idea that the alienation, metamorphosis, doubling, or transformation of the subject are expressions of unconscious desire, and cannot be accounted for as reflections or manifestations of supernatural or magical intervention, is, in fact, a fairly recent one. And these days, any author or film director who wants to present the idea of a "double" acting independently of the central "self" will probably be heavily influenced by generations of books and movies depicting the ego and id as polarities, whereas for Freud, the ego is merely a portion of the id; the duality itself can be deconstructed.

For example, in Rouben Mamoulien's 1932 version of *Dr. Jekyll and Mr. Hyde*, the protagonist is played by Frederic March, who at the time was an attractive matinee idol, and thought by some to have been inappropriately cast. March continued the popular tradition by deliberately overplaying both parts, giving Jekyll a genteel, foppish quality, in contrast to the libidinous, brutish Hyde, who presented an open defiance of all that was held dear by the Victorian ruling class. The public at large loved the film, and critics heralded it as articulating an "inescapable truth" about human nature. However, the film not only created a distinction that is not present in Freud, where ego and id support no underlying positive/negative paradigm, but, furthermore, began a new cinematic tradition, at odds with the literary source. Stevenson's novel barely alludes to Hyde's sexual nature, although this aspect of the story is one that has been developed eagerly by filmmakers. In fact, the 1920 version, which starred a leering John Barrymore, offered a wholly sexual rationale for Hyde's behavior. In the case of the original novel, however, the Jekyll–Hyde split probably had more to do with fear of the proletarian masses (in the age of Jack the Ripper) than it did with schizophrenia.

Another major tenet on which much analytic criticism of horror is based is Freud's interpretation of that "fear of awe and imaginative fear," to describe which he adopted the term "the uncanny" (*unheimlich*, literally "unhomely"). The *unheimlich* is what was once *heimisch*, familiar. The prefix "un," according to Freud, is the token of repression.

The notion of the uncanny underlies much recent horror criticism, including Barbara Creed's analysis of things that produce horror (bodily wastes, and so on) as relating to the concepts of fear and taboo. Freud himself described the uncanny as the effect of projecting unconscious desires and fears into the environment and on to other people. Frightening scenes of uncanny literature are produced by hidden anxieties within the subject, who then interprets the world in terms of his or her apprehensions. The uncanny, according to Freud, constitutes that class of the frightening that leads back to what is known of old, and long familiar. So, argues Freud, anyone who has finally rid himself of innate superstitious beliefs will be insensible to the types of uncanny feeling that arise when something actually happens in our lives to confirm old discarded beliefs, or half-conscious doubts.

The uncanny in Freud is associated with the repression of animistic taboos that, according to Freudian critics such as James Twitchell and Joseph Grixti, reemerge in the horror text in the form of a rite of passage through which the subject can overcome primal desires. Horror texts, then, apparently present fantasies of violating certain taboos (incest, necrophilia, and so on) by telling stories of ghosts, vampires, zombies, and the undead. From a Freudian perspective, such images are repressions of primary narcissism that has to be redirected by increasing social demands if we are to become acculturated, if sexual desires are to be safely abreacted into horror. Again, horror is envisaged as a discharge system for pent-up energy (which, if unreleased, threatens to implode into neurosis) so that further growth can occur.

James Twitchell takes Freud's theory of the uncanny one step further, claiming that what underlies all horror myths in our culture that are repeatedly told for more than one generation is—for no reason more specific, apparently, than that is represents a strong familial taboo—the fear of incest, and that what animates these particular myths is the fact that "beneath" the horror there is a proscriptive text detailing the social and cultural regulations of breeding. "Make-believe frights may or may not protect the audience from real scares," writes Twitchell, "but one thing they clearly do is show the consequences of socially inappropriate sexual action" (62).

Following Freud, Twitchell suggests that, since the prime audience for horror is made up of adolescents of both genders, since what we see in horror texts are often scenes of sexual confusion and frustration, and since adolescence seems characterized by a perplexity of strong drives and little knowledge, then horror texts must produce scenarios that are possible, but forbidden. Again, there is an association between uncanny events (in the fiction) and feelings (in the reader/spectator) with repressed animistic taboos—and here, specifically, with sexual confusion and frustration.

The major problem with this theory, today, is its relative impotence. At one time, incest may certainly have been more shocking than it is today, but during the last twenty years, it has been aired so frequently as a subject for media debate that it has become common knowledge, and its power of taboo seriously minimized. If all that provided the horror in horror movies were the underlying incest taboo, the resulting text would barely even be disturbing, and certainly not terrifying.

Another problem with this kind of criticism is that, whenever explanations for uncanny events or feelings are voiced *within* the text itself, they always prove something of a let-down by disappointingly "rationalizing" fascinating mysteries. At the end of *Psycho*, for example, Norman Bates's compulsive murderous transvestism is blithely "explained away" by the psychiatrist as an acute Oedipus complex coupled with sexual inadequacy stemming from intense guilt. Similar fictions always provide a rational explanation for the potentially terrifying images of horror and violence (here, for example, the nexus of ideas generated by the images of a knife, a shower, a haunted house, a stairway, an attic, and a fruit cellar), to get at a *rational* explanation for the uncanny story and the uncanny feelings it evokes in the spectator, which, once it has been proffered, means that the story, which has depended on continually effacing our sense of rationality and security, ends abruptly.

In the Joan Crawford movie *Strait-Jacket* (1964), for example, the story terminates when the director, William Castle, ties everything up in one big psychoanalytical knot, as the psychiatrist explains that transference of guilt has caused the daughter to wear her mother's clothing (plus a cheap wig and rubber mask), and imitate her murderous behavior. "When we catch sight of the psychiatrist coming out of the insane asylum to explain what we've seen," writes Twitchell, "we know the jig is up, we're off the hook" (62). Once the mysteries of the uncanny have been rationalized and anatomized by medical science, they lose their elements of intrigue and superstition, and consequently lose their potential to frighten and shock.

Another problem with Freud's reading of the uncanny is that it can never completely rationalize the images in the individual text. While it might be predicted that latency sagas be spun around a core of sexual confusion, especially reproductive anxiety, why should horror result? There is nothing intrinsically horrifying about sexuality or reproductive anxiety, nor about any eidolon of communal or familial repression. And why should different people be affected in different ways by different images and manifestations of the uncanny? And why such bizarre images—killer ants, bees, crabs, spiders, rabbits, worms, household appliances, unwanted babies, malfunctioning robots, and videocassette recorders? Critical appropriations of Freud's theories of the uncanny need to explain how the formal aspects of horror, like the formal aspects of porn, are themselves in liaison with the workings and/or the configurations of unconscious discourse in greater depth, in order to precisely analyze what exactly is embedded in the imagery of horror that is seen and unconsciously processed by the audience in such a way as to produce its particular physiological and psychological effects.

Outside of psychoanalysis, there are plenty of interesting alternative philosophical ways of reading horror texts. For example, the effects of horror could be studied in relation to Nietzsche's ideas about the body, since they seem to appeal to that same repugnant fascination, discussed by Nietzsche in *Joyful Wisdom* (1882), that prompts people to flock around a road accident or read annals of Nazi atrocities (and the notion of the sublime may also be relevant here). A lot of art seems to have this attraction, especially religious art, as many paintings of the crucifixion demonstrate, although this appeal is in the end limited, since the final effect on the mind of exposure to multiple atrocities—as Andy Warhol's printed reproductions of the electric chair suggest—is generally numbing. According to Nietzsche, horror is *experiential*, produced, and experienced by pushing the mind and body to their most extreme states, where violent horror, like sex, religious ecstasy, grief, and joy, is an essential element of life, and therefore has to be known, and savored. As

Nietzsche explains in *Joyful Wisdom*:

> The unconscious disguising of physiological requirements under the clothing of the objective, the ideal, the purely spiritual . . . I have asked myself whether philosophy hitherto has not merely been an interpreting of the body and a misunderstanding of the body . . . . (64)

Lacan's Rereading of Freud

Probably the most significant field of potential for an aesthetic evaluation of the *merits* of horror fictions emerges from Lacan's rereading of Freud. It has been important so far in this chapter to concentrate on Freudian theories of horror because Lacan himself was influenced so profoundly by Freud. Lacanian theory is a particularly relevant analyzing practice to apply to horror fictions for three reasons. First, it provides vast potential for the analysis of nontraditional media, such as comics and video; second, it has particular relevance to the body, and third, there are various associations between the mirror phase and the scopic gaze of the cinema audience.

Lacan describes the written (*l'écrit*) as the not-to-be-read, and, like Roland Barthes, he was particularly interested in other types of analysis (semiotic, semantic, structuralist) apart from just plain "reading" ("*un écrit* in my opinion is not meant to be read," wrote Lacan in *The Four Fundamental Concepts of Psychoanalysis* [24]). Non-traditional fictions, such as film, comic strips, video and similar kinds of texts thus seem particularly appropriate for the application of Lacan's rereadings of Freud.

Moreover, horror films seem to fit particularly well with Lacan's analysis of the human body, and his fascination with the corporeal. Lacan writes extensively about our individual interpretations of our own bodies, and of our bodily pleasure and pain. Like the porn movie, the horror film evinces a fascination with the human body as flesh and meat, particularly flesh and meat that is hidden from view. For example, in *The Texas Chainsaw Massacre*, when Hitchhiker slits his hand open just for the thrill of it, all the onlookers recoil in horror—except the invalid Franklin, who is fascinated by the realization that all that lies between the knowable, visible outside of the body and its secret insides is one thin membrane, protected only by a collective taboo against its violation. In her book *Men, Women and Chainsaws*, Carol J. Clover writes that "it is no surprise that the rise of the slasher film is concomitant with the development of special effects that let us see with our own eyes the 'opened body' " (31).

Clover suggests that slasher movies revolve around our witnessing body, but what we witness is another's body in experience: the body in sex, and the body in threat. "The terms 'flesh film' ('skin flick') and 'meat movie' are remarkably apt," writes Clover (31).

There are, of course, analogies to be drawn between Lacan's reading of the mirror stage and the structures of cinema itself that make Lacan's writings so crucial to cinema criticism and analysis. Kaja Silverman in her book *The Acoustic Mirror* (1988) suggests that the photograph is implicit even within the mirror stage, since here the child meets up with its own reflection through the conforming look of another. In a similar way, Annette Kuhn in *Women's Pictures* (1982) addresses the question of how cinematic meanings are constituted for viewing subjects, and suggests that the filmic state reproduces the scene of the Imaginary, and reevokes the relations of the mirror phase, implying that the filmic state is in some sense prelinguistic. This idea is implied by Lacan himself, in *The Four Fundamental Concepts of Psychoanalysis*:

> In the scopic field, the gaze is outside, I am looked at, that is to say, I am a picture. This is the function that is found at the heart of the institution of the subject in the visible. What determines me, at the most profound level, is the gaze that is outside. It is through the gaze that I enter light and it is from the gaze that I receive its effects. Hence it comes about that the gaze is the instrument through which light is embodied and through which . . . I am photo-graphed. (34)

The overall suitability of Lacanian analysis for a critical evaluation of horror fictions is nevertheless limited, mainly because many horror fictions represent a relationship between self and Other that has a sociopolitical dimension. Consequently, Lacanian and other post-Freudian theory cannot by appropriated in its entirety. Rather, the categories that are proposed here, and the distinctions that are made, are based on a few, perhaps rather isolated, of Lacan's ideas (critic Joan Copjec [1994] refers to film theory's inability to deal with anything that falls outside its carefully constructed system). Although my exposition as a whole is somewhat schematic and perhaps even oversimplified, I hope that it provides a broad frame of reference within which to place, understand, and develop popular cultural work that considers the question of audience–text relations from an aesthetic standpoint.

Critical analysts of the structures of cinevisual pleasure have fruitfully used Lacanian theory to provide various interpretations of symbolic and sexual determination. Donald Grieg, for example, discusses Hitchcock's films in terms of Lacan's theories of desire and the law, symbolic determination, and textual analysis and transgression (1989). Similarly, Pam Cook and Claire Johnston (1989) attempt to lay the foundations of a feminist film criticism by applying the theories of Lacan to film, in part because they see in Lacan's work a way of avoiding the kind of crude psychoanalytic reading limited to detecting "symptoms" or discovering sexual symbolism. Cook and Johnston also feel that a Lacanian analysis of film opens the way for a joint articulation of the physical and the social, especially in the light of Lacan's debt to Lévi-Strauss's structural anthropology.

According to the Lacanian model, the human subject is formed in relations with the world outside, which are constructed developmentally in the process of language acquisition. Freud devised his theories of the unconscious in terms of a conceptual apparatus that he forged in the face of pre-Saussurean linguistics. Lacan proceeds to a rereading of Freud in the light of various concepts produced—like the work of Bakhtin and Barthes—by and for structural linguistics, and his theories consequently involve a rejection of the vast bulk of post-Freudian psychoanalysis.

Lacan perceives the unconscious as being structured like a language, and, consequently, according to Lacan, any deciphering of unconscious discourse must abandon all misconceptions regarding the reading-selection of "symptoms," or the "sexual symbolism" discussed by Freud. Lacan reads Saussure's signifier–signified division as a metaphor for the division of the unconscious mind, which occurs in the young child between the ages of six and eighteen months—a process whereby the child ceases to identify himself with others, and comes to recognize himself as an independent being, an ego ideal. The mirror stage begins the birth of a long affair, both of love and despair, between the image and the self-image, which, as many film theorists have pointed out, finds such an intensity of expression in film, and such joyous recognition in the cinema audience. There are many similarities between cinema screen and mirror, most notably the fact that the cinema allows a temporary loss of ego while at the same time reinforcing it, and in the fact that, in the darkness of cinema, we come to "forget" the world as our ego has subsequently come to perceive it, a state which is nostalgically reminiscent of the pre-subjective moment of image recognition.

The gap between Symbolic and Imaginary orders, referred to by Lacan as the *glissage* or *béance*, manifests itself in horror films in various ways—some more obvious than others, and all interconnected—and it is from these manifestations, according to a Lacanian reading, that horror is created. Not only is the *glissage* itself a source of terror, but terror is also produced by the constant threat of its closure, leading to a fear of regression to before the mirror stage, when there was no differentiation between Self and Other. This threat of closure results in the fear of invasion from the Imaginary Order (the Other); indeed, many of the horrors in such films come from this Imaginary Order, and have their roots firmly embedded in its magical and animistic modes of thought. Paradoxically perhaps, these fears conceal a constant desire to obliterate the *glissage* by closing the gap, symbolically returning to the safety of the womb. The fact that this desire is unattainable is perhaps the most frightening horror of all. I explain this argument in more detail in the remainder of this chapter.

The Horror of *Glissage*

Many people find slasher movies to be so offensive and objectionable because these kinds of films are so much more *explicit* than traditional horror films—that is, they tend to exhibit the maximum amount of blood being spilled, bodies being cleaved and ripped asunder, open wound sequences, and visual depictions of the body's inner organs (brains, intestines, eyeballs, and so on). This *in itself* is neither particularly shocking nor especially horrible, and similar depictions can be found in most anatomical textbooks. Indeed, in certain other aesthetic contexts, the presentation of violent deaths, particularly at the expense of plot originality, can constitute the highest order of literature— consider Senecan tragedy, for example, or Samurai drama. To suggest that a horror film is *in itself* explicit, then, is hardly a valid criticism. Nor are accusations that the film is simple or superficial, since, again, in certain other aesthetic contexts, such descriptions may contain great praise—consider folk songs and border ballads, for example. Why, then, are recent of slasher films held to be so offensive, so outrageous, so deadening? In order to answer this question, it is first necessary to take a closer look at some of the films themselves.

According to Freud in *Beyond the Pleasure Principle*, humans are not gentle, but creatures among whose instinctual endowments is to be reckoned a powerful sense of aggression. This violence endemic to human subjectivity is convincingly demonstrated in the explicit nature of horror texts; a brief survey illustrates the point dramatically. The most explicit films of the 1970s and 1980s included Tobe Hooper's *The Texas Chainsaw Massacre* (1974) George Romero's *Dawn of the Dead* (1978) (see figures 6.1–6.3) and William Friedkin's *The Exorcist* (1973), all of which involved the graphic portrayal of human flesh. In December 1981,

Figure 6.1 *Dawn of the Dead* (George Romero, 1978)

Figure 6.2 *Day of the Dead* (George Romero, 1985)

Figure 6.3 *The Texas Chainsaw Massacre* (Tobe Hooper, 1974)

when the *Wall Street Journal* undertook a survey to explain why people frequented horror films, the replies often included reference to the films' "disgusting" elements as an explanation of why they give pleasure (Barker, 29).

Indeed, the explicit display of cleaven and mutilated bodies has always been a mainstay of the horror movie, ever since Tod Browning's 1932 movie *Freaks* included a brief shot of an armless, legless man crawling rapidly through the mud with a knife in between his teeth, and emerging from under a circus wagon like a gigantic worm. *Freaks* was the object of a storm of controversy when it first opened in 1932, mainly because of its use of real sideshow oddities—dwarfs, pinheads, and Siamese twins. At the end of the movie, the high-wire artist is somehow transformed into a chicken with the head of a woman.

A brief survey of explicit horror films since *Freaks* would have to include *Mark of the Devil* (1984), which presented a catalogue of atrocities and included, at least for American audiences, the offer of a free vomit bag for anyone brave enough to attend. Peter Jackson's early horror movie *Bad Taste* (1981) featured the ritual consumption of human vomit; Pasolini's *Salo*, a rendering of de Sade's *120 Days of Sodom* (1975) used excrement in a similar way; the controversial mondo movie *Circumcision* (1978) showed a Bedouin circumcision ritual, involving the flaying of human skin from the navel to the knee. This kind of horror has been endemic in literature since Seneca and Dante. For better of worse, however, recent advances in cinematic special effects have made it possible to simulate scenes of maiming or dismemberment in extraordinarily credible detail. Horror movies are the repositories of such effects; what can be done is done, and slasher movies take the greatest advantage of this potential. In *Friday the 13th III* (in 3-D, 1987), we see a human head being stepped on so that the eyes pop out; in *Friday the 13th IV* (1984) we see a decapitation scene; in *Halloween II* (1981) we see a hypodermic needle penetrating an eyeball in close-up. But why should this explicitness prove so horrifying, and so controversial?

Noel Carroll, in his book *The Philosophy of Horror* (1990), classifies such scenes as containing examples of intersitital imagery, horrifying because it defies categorization—neither inside the body nor out, neither part of the body nor wholly alien—and therefore terrifying because of its essential Otherness. A Lacanian analysis raises several similar interesting issues about the relationship between horror films, fiction, and subjectivity, leading to the conclusion that horror is held to be so offensive precisely because it leads to a dismantling of our notion of psychological coherence, and a questioning of the nature of reality itself.

Lacan's substitution of a relation between Symbolic and Imaginary Orders for the more conventional notion of a coherent, autonomous ego also includes the idea of alienation and aggression as being endemic to human subjectivity, rather than aberrations from a more stable norm. A Lacanian reading of these fantasies of deconstructed, demolished bodies—bodies that have been divided, disintegrated, and mutilated—regards them as opposing the traditional category of a unitary self. These bodies are caught in the gap between the Imaginary and the Symbolic; they are representative of neither a wholly separate, ego-centered individual, nor of a disintegrated, undifferentiated, collective identity. From a Lacanian perspective, these visions of split and broken bodies represent graphic depictions of subjects *in process*, ultimately suggesting, as in pornography, possibilities of other selves, of different histories, different bodies. These fictions are horrifying, then, because they continually reenact the division of ideal self (Symbolic Order) from primal self (Imaginary Order). They offer an implicit, subliminal depiction of the continuous and irresolute division between Imaginary and Symbolic Orders, a separation that leads to frightening feelings; as Lacan puts it, "the condition of the subject separated from the Imaginary Order bears with it a loss and yearning that register its link with the Imaginary" (41). This gap creates a sense of division, duality, absence, and silence, and from this basic pull toward entropy derive many of the thematic clusters of the horror film: obsessions with death, sex, cannibalism, and animism, and, most significantly, graphic depictions of changes of form.

According to Lacanian theory, these changes of form take place when the ego ideal is incapable of doing something that the primal self secretly desires to do. A similar paradigm may apply to schizophrenia prototypes; Norman Bates in *Psycho* dresses in his mother's clothing in order to attack and possess his victims, something that Norman himself seems otherwise incapable of doing. Similarly, in Michael Powell's *Peeping Tom* (1960)—the story of a young man who has been psychologically destroyed by his father and rendered incapable of receiving love—Mark Lewis is able to perform the murders that his anxious everyday persona finds so repulsive. Feminist critics read the blindness of Mark's girlfriend's mother as a heavy irony. According to Powell's vision, we are all voyeurs of some sort, but, free of the need to look, the woman sees more clearly than anyone, thus symbolizing the strong, caring parent that Mark never had.

This representation of *glissage* sometimes also takes the form of darkness, or subdued lighting effects, since the worrying ambiguity of dim lighting, when many of the clues normally available to us in the 3-D sphere are missing, derives from the fact that the impression of something given to us by our senses can fairly accurately be seen as referring to a variety of physical objects. This explains the dim lighting effects in the early Universal horror films, formulaic recapitulations of the German expressionist films of a decade earlier, heralded by *The Cabinet of Dr. Caligari* (1919).

The Threat of Closure

In Lacanian terms, horror fantasies have a tendency to threaten closure of the division between Imaginary and Symbolic Orders, and a return to that state coeval with the mirror phase, characterized by the lack of differentiation between self and Others. The terror that is produced by this alienating division constitutes a central part of horror fictions, and appears in a variety of forms, ultimately blurring genre divisions.

At times, fictive storyline merges with "truth"—in the mondo movie, for example. Films like the *Faces of Death* series feature out-takes of news footage too disturbing to be shown on television, generally depicting various kinds of disasters, from train wrecks to public executions and lynchings. In some cases, this footage is interspersed with hardcore pornography.

Other horror fictions dissolve genre barriers by permitting the storyline to collapse altogether. The 1975 movie *Bug*, for example, is a feature-length excuse for the moment when a cockroach crawls out of a telephone receiver, latches on to the heroine's hair, and sets fire to her brain. As in the tradition of the Grand Guignol, subtlety, plot, psychology, love interest, and so on are all sacrificed to the shock effect and prevailing themes of pain and terror. As John McCarty points out in his book *Splatter Movies* (1984):

> Splatter movies . . . steal plots from anywhere; after all, a plot is only a method of getting from one gory episode to the next . . . In their pursuit of perfect gore, splatter movies also dispense with any kind of plausibility, and minor details in particular are seldom even considered . . . (1)

Such movies create horror because they come very close to being "the Other film" that Thierry Kuntzel (1993) claims that the classic narrative film must always work to conceal. This "Other" film would be a film wherein genre barriers would collapse completely: the "protagonist" would not even find a place in the flow of the narrative; the configuration of events contained in the formal matrix would not form a progressive order; the spectator–subject would never be reassured, and so on. In its total collapse of structural conventions and genre barriers, and in its total lack of differentiation, this "Other" film would be a classic film of sustained terror, and in contemporary cinema, it is closely suggested by movies dealing with explicit horror.

The threat of closure is also suggested by the collapse of genre barriers which occurs when innovators within a genre—writers, comic book artists, or filmmakers—explore, stretch and extend the boundaries and signifying properties of the traditions within which they work. Their consistent need, like that of the makers of pornography, to test out various degrees of explicitness and thresholds of acceptability also suggests the ultimate collapse of genre barriers.

Two of the most critically reputable fictions of the 1980s were graphic novels by Alan Moore, *Swamp Thing* (1981) and *Watchmen* (1986), both of which emerged initially as monthly comics that were subsequently published in a single volume. *Watchmen* involves the reign of a new generations of superheroes in a pre-apocalyptic New York; *Swamp Thing* follows the adventures of a vegetable humanoid who can merge with trees and travel through time. This type of horror, especially in its depiction of a nonhuman protagonist, or a revision of what was originally a medium for children (the superhero comic), moves toward a dismantling of narrative conventions. For example, the concept of realistic "character" is collapsed, as is the notion of the singular, human, ego-centered individual protagonist, thus mocking and parodying a blind faith in psychological coherence. "The art of horror," writes James Twitchell, "is . . . the art of generating breakdown" (16).

E. W. Hildick, of the Comics Campaign Council, took the view that visual representation is always and necessarily inferior to the written word (1963). However, Martin Barker, in his study of the American-style comics produced in Britain during the 1950s and 1960s, argues that it is useless to profess a "moral" concern with using media which complement the traditional learning process, since such attitudes ignore the importance of visual literacy as a distinct form of learning, where pictures interact in ways that create important and interesting new ways of thinking. In fact, it is usually the illustrations that make horror comics so powerful and so memorable, and where conventional letter-ing is used (as opposed to speech and thought bubbles), it is used in new, illustrative ways whose impact is sometimes oblique. For example, when the crypt-keeper cackles his introductions to the stories in *Tales from the Crypt*, the most horrible details are capitalized, just as they are in the subsidiary slogans for George Romero's (1968) *Night of the Living Dead* ("They keep coming back in a bloodthirsty lust for HUMAN FLESH!"). If, as Lacan argues, "every word indicates the absence of what it stands for," and man is caught "in the rails of metonymy," then the horror comic, like the tabloid newspaper and the pornographic maga-zine, is an especially powerful means of communication.

The Threat of Invasion

From a Lacanian point of view, many horror texts can be read as threats of the invasion of our own selfish, ego-centered space by the Other of the Imaginary Order, with its absence of all differentiations, leading to the obliteration of the self as we know it. This fear of invasion is prefig-ured in the horror genre, as it is in pornography, by stories of possession, infestation, penetration, irruption, fusion, fission, and so on. In demon possession movies like *The Exorcist*, for example, the elimination of the self is figured through the invasion of the psyche by the demonic Other. Audiences predisposed to the idea of a true devil, and the reality of possession, generally reacted strongly to the studied tone and general air of importance that surrounded *The Exorcist*, a film in which the division between the body and what is outside of the body collapses completely; the alien Other is allowed to enter the confines of the body, and, in doing so, effects a radical transformation, both physical and spiritual.

Certainly, a thematic development in horror fictions of the last thirty years has to do with the often literal invasion of our personal space or body by someone or something from far away. This invasion is made more terrible when our personal space is particularly vulnerable—in conditions of nakedness, for example. The shower scene in *Psycho* is especially shocking, not just because of the blood streaming down the drain or the virtuoso camera work, but because Marion Crane is all the time completely naked. Similarly, the possession scenes in *The Exorcist* are particularly frightening because the possessed body is that of a young child.

This threat of obliteration has also given rise to a spate of what have been labeled "paranoia" movies, in which the source of horror is simply a formless sense of unease. The "paranoia" text has basically the same genesis as the "possession" text, although its direction is somewhat different. Whereas the "possession" text rereads the lines of the Gothic horror text and the myths of Freudian depth psychology for imagery and storyline, the "paranoia" fiction looks outside, to whatever national threat is current in the newspapers and on television. For example, Stephen King writes "paranoia" stories, always with a contemporary setting, which consistently attempt to reread the traditional themes and images of horror in terms of the paranoid anxieties—or, as King terms them in his book *Danse Macabre*—the "phobic pressure points" of the contemporary Western psyche as he sees it.

The most successful horror texts couch their threats in some ostensibly unthreatening, familiar, everyday shape, effecting a disturbing transformation of familiar into unfamiliar. The 1965 British horror movie *The Lift*, for instance, spotlights an everyday object of which people are subliminally afraid (the elevator), and turns it into a monstrous machine with a mind and a life of its own, waiting to invade our lives and their order with its nonhuman, nonmaterialistic rationality (as Freud's work on "Gradiva" has shown, the uncanny seems to blur the divide between animate and inanimate). Similarly, Stephen King's 1983 novel *Cujo*—the story of a St. Bernard dog that inexplicably turns rabid and takes a kind of "moral" revenge on his keepers by terrorizing the adulterous wife, while allowing the faithful husband to go unmolested—is meant to both prod and symbolize the "phobic pressure points" of social and psychological dimensions.

In horror texts, uncanny automata, mechanical dolls, ventriloquists' dummies, and machines out of control, all become powerful metaphors for the rigidity of the existing Order, and either its collapse, or its invasion by another kind of Order. Horror arises, writes Joseph Grixti, when there is doubt about the (customarily assumed) security of habitual reality. These horrors of possession and invasion threaten all aspects of the Symbolic Order and imply, finally, that the ego ideal (that is, we ourselves), might be totally eliminated by the Imaginary. These different representations of the Other in horror and porn lead to a dismantling of ideas about psychological coherence, demonstrating the pertinence of Lacan's critique of the unitary self.

Traditional horror fictions generally present an "outside" threat intending to "take over" and possess the victim—the vampire is from Transylvania, the mummy from Egypt, the ghoul from the Middle East, and the zombie from the Caribbean. "The Thing" is always from "Another World" (cf. *The Thing from Another World* [1951] and its hi-tech remake by John Carpenter, *The Thing* [1982]). Even in *Invasion of the Body Snatchers* (1956) and *Night of the Living Dead* (1968), we are told that the "pods" and "radiation" come from "outer space."

In the most frightening types of paranoia movies, however, the threat is located not in a rabid St. Bernard or an uncontrollable electric elevator, but in the entire Western value-system itself. Many horror movies situate their horrors inside the middle-class value systems they terrify. Joseph Grixti attempts to explain this tendency by suggesting that the horror genre is best understood as a language "related to fear and uncertainty," which is an expression (rather than a primary cause) of an undesirable or "unsatisfactorily patched-up" state of society (147–148). Most commonly, this "state of society" is the nuclear family. One of the main targets for the Comics Campaign Council, according to Martin Barker, was a carefully drawn tale of Western middle-class familial horrors called "The Orphan," the story of a cunning eight-year-old girl who shoots her father in bed, frames her mother and her mother's lover for the murder, and, in the end, gets them both sent to the electric chair so she is able to live with a kindly stepmother.

In *The Exorcist*, the film's catalogue of miserable parent–child relationships provides a believable and distressing context for the supernatural mayhem (Reagan's parents are divorced, her father neglects her, and Father Karras's mother dies in poverty). In George Romero's highly celebrated zombie epic *Night of the Living Dead*, a hint of incest adds to a growing sense that all family ties are becoming hopelessly confused. As James Twitchell puts it:

> . . . the daughter, Karen, has been nipped by a zombie and her parents, unwilling to believe that she will share the same destiny as the other victims, take her down to the cellar . . . [where] she proceeds to feed on her wounded father and kill her still-protective mother. (72)

There is a suggestion in *Night of the Living Dead* that, in less repressive conditions, the violation of Western family taboos is a natural human desire.

In *The Exorcist*, if the family can hold together in spite of everything, the evil entity will die; if the family collapses, the evil will have stabbed successfully at the heart of society. More recent movies, however, go even further. In George Romero's *Dawn of the Dead* (1978), the *Alien* movies (1978, 1986, 1992, 1997) and John Carpenter's *The Thing* (1982), the Other seeks complete identity with humanity, looking to support it with its own evil presence. In these films, the Other probes deeper; it invades our most private spaces, impressing itself more and more indelibly on its hosts. What such horror texts ultimately illustrate is that the threat to the ego ideal comes not from "outside," but, in fact, from somewhere much closer to home. The ultimate threat to the Symbolic Order comes from within the human mind itself.

Horrors of the Imaginary Order

Certain types of collective nightmares form part of the threatening Other; they remind us of the time coeval with the mirror stage, thus articulating long-forgotten truths. These horror fictions are particularly disturbing because they remind us of our early childhood, characterized, according to Lacan, by the inability to make any distinction between Self and Others. These kinds of stories can be read as artifacts that disintegrate notions of ego, since they emerge from the Imaginary Order, the cultural unconscious that preexists the splitting of the subject. They represent a particularly nightmarish kind of homecoming; they represent "la chambre des rêves," where, writes Lacan, "je suis chez moi."

These horror texts enact an arrangement of images of sex and violence tapped straight from the unconscious to evoke without comment the nostalgias and naivétès of childhood. According to Lacan, the dynamics of this kind of primal fiction can only be understood as dreaming with the eyes open, as dreamwork made real, as "the cinèma vérité" of the psyche, as James Twitchell calls it (73); public fascination with these kinds of fictions, like public fascination with pornography, will probably continue until we manage to resolve whatever it is within us that is left unresolved by these myths.

Often, these primal stories turn out to be particularly explicit versions of old myths, nursery rhymes, folk songs, and fairy tales. Sabine Büssing, in her study of the role of the child in horror fictions (1987), finds it interesting to examine how writers of horror fiction—whether presupposing a direct relationship between the genres or not—make use of ancient fairytale motifs, and thus gives them new functions and meanings. George Pumphrey (1964), the leading campaigner of the Comics Campaign Council, described one strip to which he took particular offense as "an extraordinarily repulsive version of Hansel and Gretel, with one likable character, whom the two children push into the oven and burn to death" (66). The November 1982 issue of *Twisted Tales* included cleverly distorted versions of Hansel and Gretel, Goldilocks and the Three Bears, Little Red Riding Hood, and Jack and Jill.

A similar dynamic seems to be at work in the horror film. According to Robin Wood, *The Texas Chainsaw Massacre* works as a kind of inverted fairy tale. A group of teenagers lost in the woods stumble across an old shack full of macabre details. A chicken hangs from a cage on the ceiling; armchairs are made out of human arms; corpses swing on rocking chairs. The shack is inhabited by a cannibal family of lunatics (and their half-dead grandfather) who dress in the skins of their victims. One by one, the teenagers all either get carved to pieces by the chainsaw or hung on a meat hook, except for one girl, Sally, who survives her ordeal and escapes back into civilization and "reality." Wood suggests that *The Texas Chainsaw Massacre*, in its use of fairytale themes and motifs and its preoccupation with the family, "achieves the force of authentic art . . . As a 'collective nightmare,' it brings to focus a spirit of negativity, an undifferentiated lust for destruction that seems to lie not far beneath the surface of the modern collective unconscious" (8–9).

Freud writes that we attribute an uncanny quality to images such as these, that seem to confirm the animistic mode of thinking in general. It is quite possible to read certain horror texts, which use recurrent fairytale themes, as emerging from that state which for Jung compromises the totality of all psychic processes, conscious as well as unconscious. These images and motifs—the family, grandparents in particular, the lost child, the terrible house, murder, cannibalism, magic, giants ogres monsters, the escape or "waking up" into reality—like Jungian archetypes, manifest themselves in bizarre and extravagant fashion, and seem to exist in what Lacan describes as the "hommelettian" stage of civilization. Through their dismantling of the ideal ego and ideas of psychological coherence, these kinds of horror texts are frightening because they suggest a cultural unconscious that preexists the splitting of the subject.

The Desire for Closure

The representation of the *glissage* between Imaginary and Symbolic Orders seems to inspire, paradoxically, the desire for closure, and for the gap to be healed. Lacan has described this longing for unity as one of the most profound desires of the human subject, referring to it as "an eternal and irreducible human desire . . . an eternal desire for the non-relationship of zero, where identity is meaningless" (191), analogous to "a mystical quest for union with an absolute other" (191).

The drive to look is, according to Freud, one of the sexual or libidinal drives—a desire, that is, which operates through the play of pleasure in being looked at. Laura Mulvey points out that the scopophilic instinct (pleasure at looking at another person as an erotic object) and, in contradistinction, the ego libido (forming identification processes) act as the formations and mechanisms that cinema plays on, and that, in the darkness of the movie theater, allow us to "forget" the world as our ego has subsequently come to perceive it—a state that is nostalgically reminiscent of the pre-subjective moment of image recognition. From a Lacanian perspective, the look of desire experienced by the absorbed moviegoer is tainted by the same problem suffered by Mark Lewis in *Peeping Tom*—the voyeur's displaced and aggressive sexual excitement, the desperate impulse toward a closure of the division between the regarding and the regarded.

However, this desire is often thwarted by the structures of the text itself. Tania Modleski (1984) has pointed out that it is the fashion in many recent horror movies to radically invert and contradict the consumer's scopophilic gaze of desire by engaging in "an unprecedented assault on all that bourgeois culture is supposed to cherish" (5), including the ideological apparatuses of the family, the media, school, the mall, and so on:

> In some of the films, the attack on contemporary life strikingly recapitulates the very terms adapted by many culture critics. In George Romero's *Dawn of the Dead*, the plot involves zombies taking over a shopping center . . . and in David Cronenberg's *Videodrome*, video itself becomes the monster . . . (5)

Moreover, because the systematic breakdown of genre barriers in horror fiction often results in the dissolution of conventional models of plot as well as distinctions between "fiction" and "reality," then victims and villains, as Modleski points out, are shadowy, undeveloped characters, and are portrayed equally unsympathetically, so that narcissistic identification on the part of the audience becomes increasingly difficult. Consequently, the desire to close the *glissage* between ourselves as subjects, and the story unfolding on the screen in front of us, is attained in another way: through the dynamics of camp.

Modleski goes on to suggest that certain horror films elicit a camp style of anti-narcissistic identification that the audience delights in indulging, just as we delight in having our expectations of closure frustrated. It is not unusual at showings of films like *The Exorcist* or *The Texas Chainsaw Massacre*, to experience the audience ritualistically cheering on the devil, or encouraging the chainsaw-wielding Leatherface's mutilation of their peers. As I describe in chapter 4, George Romero's *Dawn of the Dead*—a film that features zombies taking over a shopping mall, who continue to shop compulsively amid flashing lights and piped muzak, mesmerically loading their carts full of household goods—swiftly became a midnight favorite at shopping malls all across the United States.

This "perverse" response is cleverly heralded in the film's prequel, *Night of the Living Dead*, where various family members gather round the television set, hoping for information about the apocalypse surrounding them. Gradually, they are lulled by their role as observers, and begin to sink into a relaxed enjoyment of the television show, almost oblivious to the horrors around them, until the electricity suddenly fails, and reality returns. This parody of the movie's audience as a set of mindless zombies encourages a kind of anti-narcissistic identification, in which the audience empathizes with the enemy.

There is nothing intrinsically wrong with a film simply because it concerns zombies and vampires, or because it shows explicit representations of violent deaths, or because it sacrifices storyline for the benefit of graphic effect, or because it considers style or action more important than content. Nevertheless, there is a significant sense in which the horror genre is regarded as second-rate, as cheap and low, and, as such, it attracts a highly positive, almost worshipful response from a whole host of its followers. Those audience members and critics who *praise* horror fictions generally do so because they are so easily assimilated into the ranks of camp.

The essence of camp, according to Susan Sontag in her famous essay on the subject (1967), is its love of the unnatural—of artifice and exaggeration, qualities in which films like *Bug* abound:

> Camp is a certain mode of aestheticism. It is *one* way of seeing the world as an aesthetic phenomenon. That way, the way of camp, is not in terms of beauty, but in the degree of artifice, or stylization . . . (277)

Camp, according to Sontag, is a different kind of aesthetic system, which allows contexts for the discovery of powerful and positive elements in texts ordinarily dismissed as "bad" and "low" in other aesthetic contexts. "Camp," writes Sontag, "is the consistently aesthetic experience of the world. It incarnates a victory of 'style' over 'content,' and consequently, the connoisseur of camp finds a rare and specialized kind of pleasure in the 'coarsest, commonest' arts, the 'arts of the masses' " (289). Camp, according to Sontag, asserts that good taste is not simply good taste—"hat there exists, indeed, a good taste of bad taste" (289). Still, the notions of "good taste" and "bad taste," as well as "coarse," "common," and "mass," are essentially subjectivist terms, made from within a strictly limited, conservative aesthetic context with its all-constricting polarities of "common" and "rare," "coarse" and "refined," "mass" and "elite."

Lacan's *The Four Fundamental Concepts of Psychoanalysis* is devoted in part to the topic of the subject's narcissistic gaze of desire, or *le regard*. Rather than associating the gaze, as Freud would, with the instinctual drive, Lacan describes it as a product of the subject's acknowledgment of the gap between Imaginary and Symbolic, and the desire to heal that gap:

> The sexual drive is . . . deflected from the child's primal object, the mother, into seeking an object always out of reach, to be found only by discovering its trace as an absence in every signifier. This signifying process comes to affect all looking, every recognition at once a finding and a failure to find . . . (117)

Horror fictions often introduce a new kind of perverse, camp, anti-narcissistic gaze, where the audience identifies not with the protagonist of the fiction, but with the antagonist. Nevertheless, their desire remains unsatisfied as long as the gap between Imaginary and Symbolic remains unfulfilled. In horror fictions, this consistent lack of closure can itself lead to the production of terror.

Unattainability and Occlusion

Of course, if horror fictions ever reached the *end* of the desire they intimate, they would cease to exist, since desire cannot exist without a gap between satisfaction sought, and satisfaction obtained. The chain of desire is unending, and the gaze eternally unsatisfied. From the suggestion that this gap can never be closed, and a comforting oblivion never reached, arise the ultimate horrors. Nevertheless, this suggestion remains merely a suggestion, and is never made explicit. Horror depends on occlusion, on never revealing the full truth, on not being able to know enough, and therefore what makes horror fictions so powerful is that the audience is always kept from complete knowledge, held in what James Twitchell describes as "an almost hypnogogic state of suspended belief, in dreamland, in the dark" (26).

What makes horror so disturbing, therefore, is not its potential for releasing some "latent" urges and desires, nor its presentation of an uncivilized id lurking beneath a civilized ego, nor its graphic presentations of bodies being cleaved or blood being spilt, but in its depiction of the gap between Imaginary and Symbolic Orders, and in its intimation that the desire to heal this gap is ultimately unattainable.

Most forms of popular culture, it seems, both reflect and produce a sense of desire—whether for violence and release, for sexual abandon, or for emotional satisfaction—which is replaced with the desire for "legitimate" (that is, consumer) objects of pleasure. Most forms of popular culture anticipate this sense of desire, which Lacan refers to as one of the most profound drives of the subject, describing it as eternal and irreducible. Yet rather than associating the desirous gaze, as Freud would, with the instinctual drive, Lacan describes it as a product of the subject's acknowledgment of the drive for closure. From a Lacanian perspective, the look of desire experienced by the absorbed moviegoer represents the voyeur's displaced and aggressive sexual excitement, an impulse that is always thwarted by the structures of the text itself.

Yet the fact that this desire is unattainable is never completely realized. Horror always contains something that is hidden, something still and ever-concealed, some forbidden knowledge, a kept secret. Images from horror texts are terrifying because they block our attempts to classify, categorize, and hence control them. In *Danse Macabre*, Stephen King suggests that "the very basis of the horror story" is made up of "secrets left untold and things best left unsaid" (60). In a way, this Lacanian reading of horror questions the reality of the Symbolic Order itself, and hence the "reality" of all human thoughts, beliefs, and emotions. This questioning is subtly prefigured in H. P. Lovecraft's principal theme, that "the most merciful thing in the world" is "the inability of the human mind to correlate all its contents" (42), a version of the old horror movie motif, "there are some things man was simply not meant to know."

Afterword

Common assumptions about the worth and value of "high" and "low" cultures often restrict a variety of popular forms from being included in a traditionally rather narrow cultural canon. In the preceding chapters of this book, I have attempted to demonstrate that many popular cultural forms, often characterized by their apparent failure to "stand up" to conventional critical and cultural analysis, are nevertheless interesting, mainly for their capacity for "breaking down" language and meaning into infinite layers of dialogic strata.

The pleasures contained by "low" culture are widely diverging, but they are full of comedy, humor, and irony, suggesting that these forms are profanely productive and deathless, infected with the spirit of process and inconclusiveness, and liable to break up the otherwise often grim atmosphere of "conventional" culture and society. Many forms of "low" culture, as I have attempted to explain, contain a carnivalesque creativity and vitality far from fatalism and pessimism, and it is this basic force of pleasure that gives these cultural forms their great power, and affirms the ways they link the real and the textual, discourse and desire, the spectacle, the gesture, and the body.

"Low" culture plays out the juncture of the word and the world, and interacts with both to transform not only word and world, but also author, reader, consumer, spectator, and subject of desire, who are all, between them, responsible for this transformation. "Low" culture affirms the primal connections between folklore and tradition, between heroism, simplicity, and timelessness, between Otherness and its challenge to institutionalized forms. It also affirms the ways in which play, show, and desire can destroy epic distance and free the individual consciousness from canonical practices and traditions. It seems clear to me that many forms of "low" culture have frequently been misrepresented and underestimated as products of great complexity of appeal.

My main interest in "low" culture involves a consideration of how such culture functions as a source of aesthetic pleasure. Nevertheless, during the preceding chapters, I have frequently referred to value judgments that involve moral or ideological components. Indeed, most existing criticism on "low" culture is, in one way or another, ideological—partly because subjectivity is formed through the entrance into language and culture, and partly because it is impossible to separate the pleasures produced by these texts from the social and ideological determinants of popular culture. Moreover, the pleasures produced by a lot of the popular texts I refer to either contain, or allude to, a series of cultural or countercultural class (and other) struggles, and their implications of radical social change often present a challenge to institutionalized cultural forms.

Bakhtin, Barthes, and Lacan make the case that a given culture organizes the world according to given practices, and therefore considers different aspects of the world as pertinent. All three theorists take it for granted that the relationship between language, literature, culture, and subjectivity is and always has been ambiguous. They also endorse the view that culture endows the world with meaning and significance by organizing it into categories and circumstances—such as "high" and "low" culture—which are not "naturally" present, but which represent the interests, values, and behaviors of different human communities. Bakhtin, Barthes, and Lacan acknowledge the importance of popular culture not only as a fruitful area of study, but also as an intrinsic part of human life. All three theorists allow for the type of analysis of popular texts that considers the ways in which their particular system of formations presents an alternative version of what we have come to refer to as "culture."

Many of the ideas and theories outlined by Bakhtin, Barthes, and Lacan also figure within the kind of terrain described by postmodern theorists. Critics like David Harvey, Dick Hebdige, and Andrew Ross, in their work on popular culture, also address many of the problems described earlier by Bakhtin, Barthes, and Lacan, and recover much of the territory already covered by them. Refusing, like Bakhtin, to take either the author or the artifact too seriously, postmodern theory replaces culture as an object of contemplation with culture as a means of communication. Postmodern theory analyzes the independent, interdependent battle and play at different levels and layers of modern cultural forms that, like Bakhtin's theory of polyglossia, acknowledges in each text a variety of meanings, interpretations, and subtexts. As with Lacan, postmodern theory's concern with ideas about possession, infestation, irruption, fusion, fission, and so on ultimately blurs genre barriers, obliterating traditional distinctions between the commercial and the popular, between the consumer-based, money-making designs of mass capitalist culture and the autonomous, noncommercial artifacts of "high" culture. Postmodern theory also shares Barthes's obsessions with the process of the transaction itself, "trash" theory and "low" culture. Like capitalism, postmodern art and literature replaces the "real" with a theoretical representation whose emphasis on surface and packaging is related to the notion of "newness." Postmodern artists and writers like Andy Warhol and Marcel Duchamp have, like Roland Barthes, shown a great deal of fascination with the vast area of commercial naming and lettering, and the iconography of the marketplace. Postmodern art and literature is based not on intellectual or theoretical abstraction but, like the work of Barthes, Bakhtin, and Lacan, on the rediscovery of a culture's connection to the concrete, the fusion of text and performance, the merging of the textual and the lived.

Though I have been working by a very different route, the conclusion I have reached in this book is, in fact, quite close to the work of other writers on popular culture, especially that of ideological theorists such as Rachel Bowlby and Meaghan Morris. I believe there are a range of different kinds of responses to popular cultural texts, ranging from suspicion and dismissal, to joy and delight, to an unrestrained hedonism. The most frequent consumer response, however, seems to be a kind of *desire*. The pleasures of sexual and emotional abandon suggested by porn movies, horror films, football, style magazines, and stories in the tabloids are replaced by the shopper's "legitimate" (that is, consumer) objects of desire, which can never quite fill this fundamental lack—a simultaneous arousal and frustration of desire which occurs via the process of commodity fetishism.

This chain of desire/frustration is unending. If these forms of popular culture ever reached the *ends* of the various desires they intimate and envisage, they would cease to exist, since desire cannot exist without lack, without a gap between satisfaction sought, and satisfaction obtained. This gap can never be closed, and the lack of subjectivity of a final, comforting oblivion can never be reached. Significantly, this need to attain closure, to discover an *end* to desire, is analogous to the classic Lacanian scenario of the subject's constant desire to heal the gap between the Symbolic and Imaginary Orders, the desire for merging or fusion. The subject–spectator or consumer of modern popular culture is split; the original object of desire has been lost, and can never be reclaimed. Instead, we have language, but language cannot replace repressed desire. Instead, it becomes a symbol to us of what is no longer present, and what can no longer be found.

All human desire, then, is a fetish substitution for the illusion of a "real thing," whatever that may be, or have been. The pleasures suggested by the scenarios contained in popular cultural texts are, in the end, nothing more than mystifications and misrecognitions of what Kaja Silverman refers to as "lost objects and mistaken subjects." Inevitably, in a commodified society, our desires will be displaced toward commodities, since the commodity form is the only way of dealing with desire within capitalism. These popular cultural forms, I believe, render very explicit the psychic structures of capitalist society, and of desire itself.

Sometimes, as in the case of porn movies, this interminable desire for closure may be thwarted by the perverse structures of the popular text itself, which seems to encode the message that the end of all adult desire is ultimately unattainable, and the gap between Symbolic and Imaginary Orders can never be closed. I would argue that this tendency is part of the power contained by each of these commodified popular cultural forms. Moreover, all contain a constant potential for cultural critique in their direct appeal to the inner psychic structure of our commodified desires—themselves part of the unconscious, itself formulated through our entry into culture, and into language.

The forms of popular culture I have analyzed in this book can and indeed do provide a certain amount of *jouissance*. Essentially, however, the attainment of the most heightened forms of *jouissance* involves a complete (and incompatible) lack of subjectivity, which is the end of all human desire. As it is precisely *because* the pleasures of these popular cultural forms speak to this essential human paradox that the moments of actual pleasure they represent can be attained—though always, by their very nature, only fleetingly, for a few brief moments of joy.

NOTES

Chapter 1   Carnival and Chronotope: Bakhtin and
Style Magazines

1. The authorship of several key works is disputed, and I refer in this chapter only to those works which include Bakhtin's name on the title page.
2. In their glossary to *The Dialogic Imagination*, Michael Holquist and Caryl Emerson note that Bakhtin renders both *polyglossia* and *heteroglossia* with the Russian word *raznorecie, raznorecivost'*.
3. See Michael Holquist's reference to Bakhtin's "Discourse and the Novel," in "Introduction" to *The Dialogic Imagination*, p. xix, hereafter referred to as I.
4. For some good examples of this type of language in recent literary theory, see Kroker and Cook.
5. Such areas, of course, can be separated only insofar as Bakhtin's theory of generic wholes permits, since all borders, according to Bakhtin, have already been crossed and no "zone" is ever separate.
6. In fact, these are "styles" rather than "genres." Bakhtin describes the novel as a "stylistics of genre" and can never reconcile the idea of genre with the idea of style, redeeming *genre* as a term for describing "finished and resolved wholes" and *style* as designating the syntactic and lexical patterns of identifiable social voices.

Chapter 2   Joyful Mayhem: Bakhtin
and Football Fans

1. I have found it necessary in this chapter to engage in a male gendered practice; even though I write as a woman, I have deliberately used the male pronoun throughout.

Chapter 3   Rumor, Gossip, and Scandal: Barthes and
Tabloid Rhetoric

1. For an astute example of this kind of interpretation, see Jeremy Seabrook's essay "Anatomy of a Sex Romp" in Richard Sheppard, *New Ways in Germanistick*, New York: Berg, 1990.

Works Cited

Adorno, Theodore W., *The Culture Industry—Selected Essays on Mass Culture*, London and New York: Routledge, 1991, 2001. Orig. 1972.

Alloway, Lawrence et al., *Modern Dreams—The Rise and Fall and Rise of Pop*, Cambridge, MS and London: M.I.T. Press, 1988.

——, *American Pop Art*, New York: Macmillan, 1974.

Ang, Ien, ed., *Watching Dallas: Soap Opera and the Melodramatic Imagination*, London: Methuen, 1985.

——, *Living Room Wars—Rethinking Media Audiences for a Postmodern World*, New York and London: Routledge, 1996.

Bakhtin, Mikhail M., *Problems of Dostoyevsky's Poetics*, trans. Caryl Emerson, Minneapolis: University of Minnesota Press, 1984.

——, *Rabelais and His World*, trans. Hélène Iswolsky, Bloomington: Indiana University Press, 1984.

——, *Speech Genres and Other Late Essays*, Austin: University of Texas Press, 1986.

——, *The Dialogic Imagination*, ed. and trans. Michael Holquist and Caryl Emerson, Austin: University of Texas Press, 1988. Includes "Discourse in the Novel" (DN), "Epic and Novel—Towards a Methodology for the Study of the Novel" (EN), "From the Prehistory of Novelistic Discourse" (PN).

Banham, Reyner, *Theory and Design in the First Machine Age*, Cambridge, MS and London: M.I.T Press, 1980.

Barker, Martin, "How Nasty are the Nasties?" New Society 66 (1983): 231–235.

——, *A Haunt of Fears—The Strange Case of the British Horror Comics Campaign*, London and Sydney: Pluto Press, 1984.

——, *Comics: Ideology, Power and the Critics*, Manchester, U.K.: Manchester University Press, 1989.

Barthes, Roland, *Writing Degree Zero* [1953, Paris Editions de Seuil], trans. Annette Lavers and Colin Smith, New York: Hill and Wang, 1968.

——, *Mythologies* [1957, Paris: Editions de Seuil], trans. Annette Lavers, London: Jonathan Cape, 1972.

——, *Elements of Semiology* [1964, Paris: Editions de Seuil], trans. Annette Lavers and Colin Smith, New York: Hill and Wong, 1977.

——, *Criticism and Truth* [1966, Paris: Editions de Seuil], trans. Katrine Pilcher Keunemann, London: Athlone Press, 1987.

——, *S/Z: An Essay* [1970, Paris: Editions de Seuil], trans. Richard Miller, New York: Hill and Wang, 1974.

Barthes, Roland, *The Pleasure of the Text* [1973, Paris: Editions de Seuil], trans. Richard Miller, New York: Noonday Press, 1975.

——, *Image, Music, Text*, trans. Stephen Heath, New York: Hill and Wang, 1977.

——, *New Critical Essays*, trans. Richard Howard, New York: Hill and Wang, 1980.

Baudrillard, Jean, *Idées*, Paris: Gallimard, 1976.

——, *Selected Writings*, ed. Mark Poster, Stanford: Stanford University Press, 2001.

——, *Crystal Revenge*, London: Pluto/Semiotext(e), 1990.

——, *Simulacra and Simulation*, trans. Sheila Faria Glaser, Ann Arbor: University of Michigan Press, 1994.

Bell, Daniel, *The Cultural Contradictions of Capitalism*, New York: Basic Books, 1976.

Bellour, Raymond, "Psychosis, Neurosis, Perversion," in Penley, 1988.

Benjamin, Walter, *Illuminations*, New York: Schocken, 1969.

——, *The Arcades Project*, trans. Howard Eiland and Kevin McLaughlin, ed. Rolf Tiedmann, Cambridge, MS: Belknap Press, 1999.

Bennett, Tony, *Outside Literature*, London and New York: Routledge, 1990.

Bergstrom, Janet, "Alteration, Segmentation, and Hypnosis: Interview with Raymond Bellour—An Excerpt," in Penley, 1988.

Best, Steven and Douglas Kellner, *The Postmodern Turn*, New York: Guilford, 1997.

——, *The Postmodern Adventure—Science, Technology and Cultural Studies at the Third Millenium*, New York: Guilford, 2001.

Bloom, Allan David, *The Closing of the American Mind*, New York: Simon and Schuster, 1987.

Bowlby, Rachel, *Just Looking—Consumer Culture in Dreiser, Gissing and Zola*, London: Methuen, 1985.

——, *Shopping with Freud*, London: Routledge, 1993.

Brantlinger, Patrick, *Crusoe's Footprints: Cultural Studies in Britain and America*, New York and London: Routledge, 1990.

Brooks, Peter, *Reading for the Plot—Design and Intention in Narrative*, Oxford and New York: Oxford University Press, 1984.

Carroll, David, *Paraesthetics: Foucault, Lyotard, Derrida*, New York: Methuen, 1987.

Carroll, Noel, *The Philosophy of Horror, or, Paradoxes of the Heart*, New York and London: Routledge, 1990.

Cendrars, Blaise, *Modernities and Other Writings*, trans. Esther Allen, ed. Monique Chefdor, Lincoln, NA: University of Nebraska Press, 1992.

Chomsky, Noam, *Towards a New Cold War: Essays on the Current Crisis and How We Got There*, New York: Pantheon, 1982

——, *Media Control: The Spectacular Achievements of Propaganda*, New York: Seven Stories Press, 2002.

Christian-Smith, Linda K., *Becoming Feminine: The Politics of Popular Culture*, London: Falmer, 1988.

——, "Gender, Popular Culture and Curriculum: Adolescent Romance Novels as Gender Text," *Curriculum Inquiry* 17.4 (1987): 365–406.

——, *Becoming a Woman through Romance*, New York: Routledge, 1990.

Cixous, Hélène and Catherine Clément, *The Newly Born Woman*, trans. Betsy Wing, Minneapolis: Minneapolis University Press, 1986.

Clover, Carol J., "Her Body, Himself: Gender in the Slasher Film," *Representations* 20: 187–228, 1987.

——, *Men, Woman and Chainsaws: Gender in the Modern Horror Film*, Princeton, NJ: Princeton University Press, 1993.

Cook, Pam and Claire Johnston, "The Films of Raoul Walsh," in Donald, 1989.

Copjec, Joan, *Read my Desire: Lacan Against the Historicists*, Cambridge, MA: M.I.T. Press, 1995.

Creed, Barbara, "Horror and the Monstrous-Feminine, An Imaginary Abjection," *Screen* 27.1 (1986): 44–70.

——, Review, Andrew Tudor, *Monsters and Mad Scientists: A Cultural History of the Horror Movie*, *Screen* 31.2 (1990): 236–242.

——,*The Monstrous-Feminine: Film, Feminism, Psychoanalysis*, NY: Routledge, 1993.

Dadoun, Roger, "Fetishism in the Horror Film," in Donald, 1989.

Deleuze, Gilles, *Essays Critical and Clinical*, trans. Daniel W. Smith and Michael A. Greco, Minneapolis: University of Minnesota Press, 1997.

Dika, Vera, *Games of Terror: Halloween, Friday 13th and the Films of the Stalker Cycle*, Fairleigh Dickinson University Press, 1990.

Doane, Mary Ann, *"Caught* and *Rebecca:* The Inscription of Femininity as Absence," in Penley, 1988.

Donald, James, ed., *Fantasy and the Cinema*, London: BFI Publishing, 1989.

Dreiser, Theodore, *Sister Carrie*, Philadelphia, PA: University of Philadelphia Press, 1981.

Dworkin, Andrea, *Pornography—Men Possessing Women*, New York: The Women's Press, 1981.

Eagleton, Terry, *The Function of Criticism: From the "Spectator" to Post-Structuralism*, London: Verso, 1984.

——, "Bakhtin, Schopenhauer, Kundera," in Hirschkop and Shepherd, 1989.

——, *Ideology: An Introduction*, London: Verso, 1991.

——, *The Ideology of the Aesthetic*, Oxford: Blackwell, 1990.

——, *After Theory*, New York: Basic Books, 2004.

Eco, Umberto, *A Theory of Semiotics*, Bloomington, IN: Indiana University Press, 1976.

——, *Travels in Hyperreality*, London and New York: Pan, Secker and Warburg, 1986.

——, *Interpretation and Overinterpretation*, ed. Stefan Collini, with Richard Rorty, Jonathan Culler, and Christine Brooke-Rose, Cambridge University Press, 1992.

Eliot, T. S., *Selected Essays, 1917–1932*, London: Harcourt, 1950.

Ellis, Bret Easton, *American Psycho*, New York: Vintage, 1991.

Ewan, Stuart. *Captains of Consciousness*, NY: Basic Books, 2001.

Fekete, John, ed., *Life After Postmodernism: Essays on Value and Culture*, New York: St. Martin's Press,1987.

Fell, John L., *Film and the Narrative Tradition*, Norman, OK: University of Oklahoma Press, 1974, 1986.

Feminist Review, eds., *Sexuality—A Reader*, London: Virago Press, 1987.

Fiske, John, *Television Culture*, London and New York: Methuen, 1987; Routledge, 1988, 1989.

Fitzgerald, F. Scott, *Tender is the Night*, New York: Penguin, 1978, 123.

Foucault, Michel, *The Order of Things: An Archeology of the Human Sciences*, New York: Routledge, 2001.

Fowler, Roger, *Language in the News: Discourse and Ideology in the Press*, New York and London: Routledge, 1991.

Freiberg, Anne, *Window Shopping: Cinema and the Postmodern*, Los Angeles: University of California Press, 1993.

Freud, Sigmund, *The Complete Psychological Works of Sigmund Freud*, trans. James Strachey, standard edition, London: Hogarth Press, 1953–1974, 16 vols.

Galtang, Johann and Mari Ruge, "The Structure of Foreign News," *Journal of Peace Research* 2 (1965): 64–91.

Gasset, Ortega y, *Revolt of the Masses*, London: W.W. Norton & Co., 1994.

Geist, Johann Friedrich, *Arcades: History of a Building Type*, Cambridge, MA: M.I.T. Press, 1983.

Geist, Christopher D., eds., *The Popular Culture Reader*, third edition, Bowling Green, Ohio: Bowling Green University Popular Press, 1975.

Goody, Jack and Ian Watt, *Literacy in Traditional Societies*, Cambridge: Cambridge University Press, 1989.

Gombillo, Maria Drudi and Teresa Fiori, *Archivi del Futurismo*, trans. Marjorie Perloff, volume 1, Rome: De Luca, 1958–1962.

Gramsci, Antonio, *Selections from Cultural Writings*, ed. Geoffrey Nowell-Smith, Harvard University Press, 1991.

Greenberg, Clement, "Avant-Garde and Kitsch," in Rosenberg and White, 1957.

Greig, Donald, "The Sexual Differentiation of the Hitchcock Text," in Donald, 1989.

Grixti, Joseph, *Terrors of Uncertainty—The Cultural Context of Horror Fictions*, London and New York: Routledge, 1989.

Haag, Ernst van den, *Capitalism: Sources of Hostility, An Anthology*, London: Crown Publications, 1979.

Hamilton, Richard, *Collected Words 1953–1982*, London: Thames & Hudson, 1983.

——, with Richard Morphet, *Richard Hamilton*, London: Tate Gallery Press, 1993.

Handke, Peter, *Kaspar*, Frankfurt am Main: Suhrkamp, 1973.

——, *Repetition*, trans. Ralph Manheim, New York: Farrar, Straus and Giroux 1988.

Hartley, John, *Understanding News*, New York and London: Routledge, 1982.

Harvey, David, *The Condition of Postmodernity*, Oxford: Basil Blackwell, 1990.

Haug, Wolfgang Fritz, *Critique of Commodity Aesthetics*, trans. Robert Brock, New York: Polity Press, 1986.

Hawkins, Joan, *The Cutting Edge: Art Horror and the Horrific Avant-Garde*, Minneapolis: University of Minnesota Press, 2000.

Hebdige, Dick, "Reggae, Rastas and Rudies," *Center for Contemporary Cultural Studies Occasional Paper* (25), Birmingham, U.K.: Birmingham University Press, 1974.

——, *Subculture: The Meaning of Style*, London: Methuen, 1979.

——, *Hiding in the Light: On Images and Things*, London and New York: Routledge, 1988.

Herbert, James, *Dark Places*, London: Ramboro, 1999.

Hildick, E. W., *Only the Best: Six Qualities of Excellence*, London: C.N. Potter, 1963.

Hirsch, E. D., *Cultural Literacy: What Every American Needs to Know*, Boston: Houghton Mifflin, 1987.

Hirschkop, Ken and David Shepherd, eds., *Bakhtin and Cultural Theory*, Manchester: Manchester University Press, 1989.

Hogan, David, *Dark Romance—Sex and Death in the Horror Film*, Jefferson, NC: McFarland, 1986.

Hoggart, Richard, *The Uses of Literacy*, Brunswick, NJ: Transaction, 1988.

Holland, Norman, *Holland's Guide to Psychoanalytic Psychology and Literature and Psychology*, Oxford and New York: Oxford University Press, 1990.

Horkheimer, Max, *Critical Theory: Selected Essays*, trans. Matthew O'Connell, London: Continuum, 1975.

Hutcheon, Linda, *Formalism and the Freudian Aesthetic: The Examples of Charles Mauron*, Cambridge, MA: Cambridge University Press, 1984.

——, *A Theory of Parody: The Teachings of Twentieth Century Art Forms*, New York: Routledge,1985.

——, *A Poetics of Postmodernism: History, Theory and Fiction*, New York: Routledge, 1988.

Irigaray, Luce, *Speculum of the Other Woman*, trans. G. C. Gill, Cornell University Press, 1985.

Iser, F. W., *Prospecting: From Reader Response to Literary Anthropology*, Baltimore: Johns Hopkins University, 1993.

Jameson, Frederic and Masao Miyoshi, *The Cultures of Globalism*, Raleigh, NC: Duke University Press, 1988.

——, *The Seeds of Time*, NY: Columbia University Press, 1994.

Jakobson, Roman, "Dear Claude, Cher Maitre," in Marshall Blonsky, ed., *On Signs*, Oxford: Basil Blackwell, 1985.

Jefferson, Ann, "Bodymatters: Self and Other in Bakhtin, Sartre and Barthes," in Hirschkop and Shepherd, eds., 1989, 179–186.

Johnson, Barbara, *The Critical Difference: Essays in the Contemporary Rhetoric of Reading*, Baltimore: Johns Hopkins University Press, 1980.

Kaplan, Cora, *Sea Changes*, New York: Verso, 1986.

Kappeler, Suzanne, "The White Brothel—The Literary Exoneration of the Pornographic," in *Sexuality: A Reader*, ed. Feminist Review, London: Virago Press, 1987, 329–335.

Kellner, Douglas, *Media Spectacle*, New York and London: Routledge 2003.

King, Stephen, *The Shining*, New York: Doubleday, 1977.

King, Stephen, *Cujo*, New York: Viking, 1981.

——, *Danse Macabre*, New York: Berkley Books, 1997.

Kipnis, Laura, *Against Love: A Polemic*, New York: Pantheon Books, 2003.

Kuhn, Annette, *Women's Pictures: Feminism and Cinema*, London: Verso, 1994.

Kristeva, Julia, *Powers of Horror*, trans. Leon S. Roudiez, New York: Columbia University Press, 1982.

Kroker, Arthur, Marilouise Kroker, and David Cook, *The Postmodern Scene: Excremental Culture and Hyper-Aesthetics*, New York: Macmillan, 1986.

——, *The Panic Encyclopedia: The Definitive Guide to the Postmodern Scene*, New York: Macmillan, 1989.

Kuhn, Annette, *Women's Pictures: Feminism and Cinema*, London: Verso, 1982.

Kuntzel, Thierry, *Thierry Kuntzel*, Paris: Galerie Nationale du jeu de palme, 1993.

Lacan, Jacques, *Ecrits—A Selection*, trans. Bruce Fink, London: W.W. Norton, 2002.

——, *The Four Fundamental Concepts of Psychoanalysis*, trans. Alan Sheridan, ed. J. Jacques-Alain Miller, intro. David Macey, London: Vintage, 1988.

Lamb, Larry, *Sunrise—The Remarkable Rise and Rise of the Best-Selling Soaraway "Sun,"* London: Papermac, 1989.

Lasch, Christopher, *The Culture of Narcissism, American Life in an Age of Diminishing Expectations*, New York: Norton, 1978, 1979.

Leavis, Queenie Dorothy, *Fiction and the Reading Public*, New York: Russell and Russell, 1965.

Lévi-Strauss, Claude, *The Savage Mind*, London: Weidenfeld and Nicholson, 1966.

——, *The Way of the Masks*, trans. Sylvia Modleski, Vancouver: Douglas and McIntyre, 1982.

Longford, Lord, *Pornography—The Longford Report*, London: Coronet, 1972.

Lull, James, *Inside Family Viewing—Ethnographic Research on Television Audiences*, London: Routledge, 1990.

——, *Media Scandals—Morality and Desire in the Popular Culture Marketplace*, New York: Columbia University Press, 1997.

Macdonald, Dwight, *Against the American Grain*, essays on the effects of mass culture, New York: Vintage, 1962.

——, *Discriminations: Essays and Afterthoughts 1938–1974*. New York: Grossman, 1975.

Macherey, Pierre and Etienne Balibar, interviewed by J. Kavanagh and T. Lewis, *Diacritics* 12 (1988): 50–58.

Macherey, Pierre, *In a Materialist Way—Selected Essays*, ed. Warren Montag, trans. Ted Stolze, New York: Verso, 1998.

MacKeith, Margaret, *The History and Conservation of Shopping Arcades*, London: Mansell, 1986.

Maitland, Barry, *Shopping Malls: Planning and Design*. London: Construction Press, 1985.

Malevich, Kasimir, "From Cubism to Futurism to Suprematism: The New Painterly Realism," in Bowlt, 1976.

Maltby, Richard, ed., *Dreams for Sale: Popular Culture in the Twentieth Century*, London: Harrap, 1989.

Mander, Jerry, *Four Arguments for the Elimination of Television*, New York: Morrow, 1978.

Marcuse, Herbert, *One Dimensional Man: Studies in the Ideology of an Advanced Industrial Society*, London: Beacon Press, 1992.

Marinetti, Filippo Tommaso, *Selected Writings*, ed. R. W. Flint and A. A. Coppotelli, New York: Farrar, Straus and Giroux, 1972.

Martin, Emily, *The Woman in the Body*, New York: Beacon Press, 2001.

McCarthy, George, *Dialectics and Decadence*, London: Rowan and Littlefield, 1994.

McCarty, John, *Splatter Movies: Breaking the Last Taboo of the Screen*, New York: Olympia Marketing Group, 1984.

McCracken, John, *Rencontres*, Paris: Images Modernes, 2000.

McLuhan, Marshall, *The Gutenberg Galaxy*, Toronto: University of Toronto Press, 1962.

McRobbie, Angela, *Postmodernism and Popular Culture*, New York and London: Routledge, 1994.

Metz, Christian, *Language and Cinema*, trans. D. J. Umiker-Sebeok, The Hague and Paris: Mouton, 1974.

Meyrowitz, Joshua, *No Sense of Place: The Impact of Social Behavior in the Age of Electronic Media*, Oxford: Oxford University Press, 1986.

Mitchell, Juliet, *Psychoanalysis and Feminism—A Radical Reassessment of Freudian Psychoanalysis*, New York: Basic Books, 2000.

Modleski, Tania, *The Terror of Pleasure—The Contemporary Horror Film and Postmodern Theory*, Madison: University of Wisconsin Press, 1984.

——, *Studies in Entertainment: Critical Approaches to Mass Culture*, Bloomington, IN: Indiana University Press, 1986.

Moi, Toril, *Sexual / Textual Politics*, New York and London: Routledge, 1985.

Moore, Alan, *The Saga of the Swamp Thing*, New York: DC Comics, 1993.

——, *Watchmen*, New York: DC Comics, 2000.

Morin, Jack, *The Erotic Mind—Unlocking the Inner Secrets of Passion and Fulfilment*, New York: Perennial, 1996.

Morris, Meaghan, *The Pirate's Fiancée: Feminism, Reading, Postmodernism*, New York and London: Routledge, 1997.

Mulvey, Laura, "Visual Pleasure and Narrative Cinema," in Penley [1887, 1908] 1988.

Nietzsche, *"On the Geneology of Morals" and "Ecco Homo,"* trans. Walter Kaufmann, New York: Vintage, 1969.

——, *Joyful Wisdom* [1882], trans. Thomas Common, New York: Frederick Ungar Publishing Co., 1971.

O'Pray, Michael, "Surrealism, Fantasy and the Grotesque—The Cinema of Jan Svankmajer," in Donald, 1989.

Orwell, George, "Boy's Weeklies," *Horizon* March 3, 1939.

Paglia, Camille, *Sexual Personae—Art and Decadence from Nefertiti to Emily Dickinson*, New York: Vintage, 1990.

Patterson, David, "Mikhail Bakhtin and the Dialogical Discussion of the Novel," *Journal of Aesthetics and Art Criticism* 44(2) (1985): 131–138.

Pechey, Graham, "Modernity and Chronotopicity in Bakhtin," in David Shepherd, ed., *The Contexts of Bakhtin*, London: Harwood Academic Press, 1998, 173–182.

Penley, Constance, ed., *Feminism and Film Theory*, London and New York: Routledge, 1988.

——, "Time Travel, Primal Scene and Critical Dystopia," in Donald, 1989.

——, *The Future of an Illusion: Film, Feminism and Psychoanalysis*, Minneapolis: University of Minnesota Press, 1989.

Postman, Neil, *Amusing Ourselves to Death: Public Discourse in the Age of Showbusiness*, London: Viking Press, 1986.

Prawer, S. S., *Caligari's Children—The Film as Tale of Terror*, London and New York: Oxford University Press, 1980.

Probyn, Elspeth, *Outside Belongings*, New York and London: Routledge, 1996.

Propp, Vladimir, *Theory and History of Folklore*, Minneapolis: University of Minnesota Press, 1985.

Pumphrey, George, *What Children Think of Their Comics*, London: Epworth Press, 1964.

Raban, Jonathan, *Soft City*, London: Harvill Press, 1998.

Radway, Janice A., *Reading the Romance: Women, Patriarchy, and Popular Literature*. University of North Carolina Press, 1991.

Redhead, Steve, *The End of the Century Party: Youth and Pop Towards 2000*, Manchester and New York: Manchester University Press, 1990.

Richards, Bernard, unpublished letter to author.

Richards, Thomas, *The Commodity Culture of Victorian England*, Stanford: Stanford University Press, 1990.

Richardson, Samuel, *Clarissa, or, The History of a Young Lady* [1748], London: Penguin Classics, 1986.

Rieff, Philip, *The Triumph of the Therapeutic—Uses of Faith After Freud*, New York: Harper and Row, 1968.

Romains, Guy, *Unamist Manifesto*, Paris: Gallimard, 1914.

Roman, Leslie G. and Linda K. Christian-Smith, *Becoming Feminine: The Politics of Popular Culture*, London: Taylor and Francis, 1988.

Rose, Jacqueline, *States of Fantasy*, Oxford and New York: Clarendon Press, 1996.

Rosenberg, Bernard and David M. White, eds., *Mass Culture: The Popular Arts in America*, Illinois: Free Press, 1957, 1964, 1965.

Sartre, Jean-Paul, *Being and Nothingness*, trans. Hazel Barnes, London, 1957.

de Saussure, Ferdinand, *Course in General Linguistics*, trans. Wade Baskin, New York: McGraw Hill, 1966.

Seabrook, Jeremy, "Anatomy of a Sex-Romp," in Richard Sheppard, ed., *New Ways in Germanistik*, New York: Berg, 1990.

Schachtman, Tom, *Inarticulate Society: Eloquence and Culture in America*, New York: Free Press, 1995.

Schiller, Herbert. *Culture, Inc.: The Corporate Takeover of Public Consciousness*. Oxford University Press, 1991.

Schoell, William, *Stay Out of the Shower—25 Years of Shocking Films Beginning with Psycho*, New York: Dembner, 1985.

Shakespeare, William, The *Tempest* [1623], Oxford: Oxford University Press, 1998.

Shepherd, David, see Ken Hirschkop.

Sheridan, Susan, ed., *Grafts*, London and New York: Verso, 1988.

Silverman, Kaja, *The Acoustic Mirror—The Female Voice in Psychoanalysis and Cinema*, Bloomington: Indiana University Press, 1988.

Sobchack, Vivian, *Screening Space—The American Science-Fiction Film*, Rutgers University Press, 1997.

Sontag, Susan, *Against Interpretation*, New York: Picador, 2001.

Soothill, Keith and Sylvia Walby, *Sex Crime in the News*, London: Routledge, 1991.

Steinem, Gloria, *Outrageous Acts and Everyday Rebellions*, London: Cape, 1983.

Stevenson, Robert Louis, *The Strange Case of Dr. Jekyll and Mr. Hyde* [1886], London: Penguin Worlds Classics, 1979.

Swingewood, Alan, *The Myth of Mass Culture*, London: Macmillan, 1977.

de Tocqueville, Alain, *Democracy in America*, ed. and trans. Harvey C. Mansfield and Delba Winthrop, Chicago: University of Chicago Press, 2000. Orig. 1835.

Thompson, E. P., *The Making of the English Working Class*, London: Macmillan, 1963, 1966.

Toderov, Tsvetan, *Introduction to Poetics*, Minneapolis: University of Minnesota Press, 1981.

Tomlinson, Alan, ed., *Consumption, Identity and Style—Marketing, Meanings, and the Package of Pleasure*, London and New York: Routledge, 1990.

Turner, Graeme, *British Cultural Studies: An Introduction*, London and New York: Routledge, 1996.

Twitchell, James, *Dreadful Pleasures*, Oxford: Oxford University Press, 1985.

Uhlig, Klaus, *Pedestrian Areas—From Malls to Complete Networks*, New York: Arch, 1991.

Volosinov, Vladimir, *Marxism and the Philosophy of Language,* trans. L. Matejka and I. R. Titunik, New York and London: Seminar Press, 1973. Orig. 1929.

Williams, Linda, "When the Woman Looks," *The Dread of Difference: Gender and the Horror Film*, Grant, B. K. ed., Austin: University of Texas Press, 1996, 15–24.

——, "Film Bodies: Gender, Genre, and Excess," *Film Theory and Criticism: Introductory Readings*, fifth edition, L. Braudy and M. Cohen, eds., Oxford: Oxford University Press 1999, 701–715.

——, *Hard Core—Power, Pleasure and the "Frenzy of the Visible,"* Berkeley: University of California Press, 1999.

Williams, Raymond, *Keywords: A Vocabulary of Culture and Society*, Oxford: Oxford University Press, 1985.

Williamson, Judith, *Decoding Advertisements, Ideology and Meaning in Advertising*, London: Boyers, 1984.

——, *Consuming Passions: The Dynamics of Popular Culture*, London: Boyers, 1986.

Willis, Susan, *A Primer for Daily Life*, New York: Routledge, 1991.

Wills, Clair, "Upsetting the Public: Carnival, Hysteria and Women's Texts," in Hirschkop and Shepherd, eds., 1989, 130–151.

Winn, Marie, *The Plug-in Drug*, New York: Viking, 1977, 1985; Penguin, 2002.

Wood, Robin, "The Return of the Repressed," *Film Comment* 14.1 (1978).

York, Peter, *Modern Times: Everybody Wants Everything*, London: Heinemann, 1984.

INDEX